UNCLE JOHN'S
STRANGE
&
SCARY
BATHROOM READER®
FOR KIDS ONLY

by the
Bathroom Readers'
Institute

Bathroom Readers' Press
Ashland, Oregon

UNCLE JOHN'S
STRANGE AND SCARY
BATHROOM READER®
FOR KIDS ONLY

For information, write:
Bathroom Readers' Institute
P.O. Box 1117, Ashland, OR 97520
www.bathroomreader.com

Cover design and illustrations by John Gaffey

Uncle John's Strange and Scary
Bathroom Reader For Kids Only
by the Bathroom Readers' Institute

ISBN-10: 1-59223-385-6
ISBN-13: 978-1592-23385-4
Library of Congress Control Number: 2005922737

Printed in the United States of America
First printing 2006
06 07 08 09 10 5 4 3 2 1

READERS' RAVES

From some of our strangest and scariest readers!

"I got one of your books for my birthday and I can't get off it my parents think I'm too nerdy for my own good but I think your books are better than words can say!"

—**Freeman**

"Your books are the best ever. EVER! My whole family loves them (even my little sister). You should do more stuff about ghosts because ghosts scare my sister."

—**Marvin**

"I'm 13 years old, and I'm a really big fan of your books. They rock!!!"

—**Rachel**

"Hey Uncle John! I love your *Bathroom Readers For Kids Only* books! I read them in the bathroom, in the car, on my bed, everywhere possible. They are HILARIOUS!! I especially like the 'gross stuff'!!"

—**Jen**

"I have all of your *For Kids Only* books and still love them even though I'm 12 years old."

—**Lexi**

"If I had to choose between *Bathroom Readers* or homework, *Bathroom Readers* would be what I would choose."

—**Wesley**

TABLE OF CONTENTS

DID YOU KNOW?

• In the United States it's illegal for anyone to have contact with extraterrestrials or their vehicles.

• Jogging with your eyes closed is illegal in Florida.

• Whistling underwater is against the law in Vermont.

• People who make ugly faces at dogs may be fined or jailed in Oklahoma.

INTRODUCTION
Tales from the BARK side

H iya Kids!
Don't be scared—it's only me, Porter the Wonder Dog. I'm wearing this disguise because Uncle John told me that ghosts can't get me if they can't recognize me (although I suspect his real rea-

son was to trick me into wearing these dorky glasses).

Before you start reading, you might want to get your own disguise. Because I warn you: There are a lot of ghosts roaming through these pages. That's not all—there are also vampires, zombies, and little green aliens with big scary eyes! (Whimper whimper.)

But if scary's not your thing, then we have plenty of strange stuff for you—there's the guy who is transforming himself into a cat, another guy whose entire body is covered with hair, and ridiculous records, weird sports, and inflatable underwear. And a whole bunch more crazy stuff, but you'll have to read it for yourself.

First though, Uncle John wanted me to thank the strange and scary humans who helped make this book: Jahnna, Malcolm, Maggie, John G., Jeff, Brian, Jay, Caitlin, Thom, and Julia. I give them all two paws up!

Until next time,

Go with the Flow!

THANK YOU!

*The Bathroom Readers' Institute thanks those
people whose help has made this book possible.*

Gordon Javna

Jahnna Beecham

Malcolm Hilgartner

John Gaffey

Jeff Altemus

Jay Newman

Brian Boone

Maggie McLaughlin

Amy Miller

Julia Papps

Thom Little

Allen Orso

Jennifer Thornton

John Dollison

Dan Schmitz

Judy Hadlock

Cheap Tricks, the
Wiseguy's Supermarket

Caitlin and McKenzie

Connie Vazquez

Raincoast Books

Banta Book Group

Terri Dunkley

Sydney Stanley

JoAnn Padgett

Dash and Skye

Scarab Media

Steven Style Group

Jennifer P. & Melinda A.

Laurel, Mana, Dylan,
and Chandra

Matthew Furber

Shobha Grace

Gideon and Sam

Porter the Wonder Dog

Thomas Crapper

*   *   *

Special thanks to Mrs. Dymond's 4th grade class:
Adam, Amber, Darby, Brett, Makena, Jarrett, John,
Tatum, Divyang, James, Lauren, Kye, Alexandria, Alex,
Sebastian, Stephen, Sydney, Lauren, Jesse, Bailey,
Megan, Alivia, Brooke, Jacob, Chloe, Bodie

CABBAGE PATCH SON
And you think your family's weird!

P at and Joe Prosey from Leonardtown, Maryland, have spent 19 years raising a Cabbage Patch doll as their only son. Kevin, as they call him, is a one-foot-tall doll, "adopted" from the Coleco toy company. "With every kid that you adopt, you promise to love them and be a good parent, and take care of this child," Pat Prosey explained. "And that's what we did with Kevin."

Their Cabbage Patch son has his own playroom, a complete wardrobe, his own pet dog, and a bright red (doll-sized) Corvette for zipping around the driveway. They've even set up a college fund for him.

The couple takes Kevin on all of their vacations. When they talk to the doll, he answers back—in a voice supplied by Joe.

The Proseys actually have a real daughter, too (her name is Vicky), but they've told reporters that Kevin is the ideal child. "He's easygoing, quiet, and well-behaved."

GAG ME WITH
A SNEAKER

*To find success, sometimes you
must meet with de-feet.*

It's official! Noah Nielsen has America's smelliest sneakers. Odor Eaters, maker of anti-foot odor products, declared Noah the winner in their 30th annual competition. Contestants came from as far away as Alaska, Texas, Washington, Arkansas, and Utah to compete, but the 10-year-old from Vermont was the winner.

Noah credits his success to "No socks, ever!" His sweaty, dirt-encrusted toes—which can be seen through the gaping holes in his Adidas—are the reason his shoes are so ripe. In fact, Noah's feet were so foul that during the competition one judge gagged and another staggered backward, crying, "Human feet shouldn't smell that bad!" But Noah just smiled because he won a $500 savings bond, a $100 check for new sneakers, and a large supply of Odor Eaters. P-U!

IF THE SHOE FITS

FEET FACTS

• Presidents George Washington, Abraham Lincoln, and Bill Clinton all wore size 13 shoes.

• Your feet can be up to 10 percent larger by the end of the day.

• What do you do when you need a little luck? According to Irish folklore, just nail a shoe to a tree. In 1996 a property owner in Bainbridge, Ohio, nailed a shoe

to his tree for luck. Before he knew it shoes of all shapes and sizes were nailed next to his. Now the tree is known far and wide as...the Shoe Tree.

BUSTED!

Charles Taylor of Wichita, Kansas, was charged with holding up a store and stealing a pair of boots worth $70. At his trial, the man pleaded "not guilty," and then took the witness stand wearing the stolen boots...with the tags still on them! (The jury found him guilty.)

MONSTER LINEUP

Thousands of people claim to have seen these creatures. Have you? Here's the scoop on America's least wanted.

MOTHMAN

Description: Stands seven feet tall. Has no head, yet has bright red eyes on top of its shoulders. Flies with featherless wings.

Behavior: Mothman screeches loudly and flies at speeds of up to 100 mph, sometimes straight up in the air like a rocket. Dogs disappear and UFOs are often sighted after an appearance.

Last Seen: Point Pleasant, West Virginia

BIGFOOT

Description: Seven to eight feet tall, weighs 300 pounds. Has reddish brown fur, long arms, and big humanlike feet.

Behavior: Bigfoot smells really bad, like a cross between a skunk and a wet dog. He is very shy so he runs away from humans, but he often leaves a strange calling card of stick structures woven into the forks of trees.

Last Seen: Lots of places, such as Northern California, Oregon, Washington, British Columbia, and Texas.

ZOMBIE

Profile: The "walking dead." Has a blank face and staggering walk and speaks very slowly.

Behavior: Zombies are corpses raised from the grave by voodoo sorcerers, or *bokors*. They become mindless slaves seeking revenge for the bokor. Only a taste of salt will release the zombie so it can return to its grave.

Last Seen: Haiti

THE JERSEY DEVIL

Description: A cross between a snake, a horse, and a bird. And it flies.

Behavior: The Jersey Devil has terrorized the Pine Barrens of New Jersey for more than 260 years. It has been seen by more than 2,000 witnesses. A terrible disaster often follows this creature's appearance.

Last Seen: New Jersey (obviously).

TOY STORIES

Here's what happens when toy makers go...weird.

THUGGIES. These dolls come with something that no dolls ever had before—criminal records. That's right, "Motorcycle Meanie," "Dickie the Dealer," and "Bonnie Ann Bribe" are all crooks who come packaged in their own jail cells. Introduced in 1993, Thuggies were designed to teach kids that crime doesn't pay.

FORWARD COMMAND POST. Grandma's dollhouse never looked like this. Imagine a two-story house that's been taken over by soldiers in a war zone, and you've got Ever Sparkle Toys' strange creation. This bombed-out dollhouse comes with broken railings, walls filled  with bullet holes, and soldiers armed with long-range sniper rifles. This 75-piece set includes high tech cannons, weapons in footlockers, explosives, camo combat gear, and an American flag. (Ages 5 and up.)

WHAT'S IN NED'S HEAD?

Ned's Head is a stuffed
plush head filled with
gross plastic
things—fake
vomit, moldy
cheese, rats,
spiders,
worms, and
more. Kids
compete by
fishing the yucky
stuff out of Ed's ears, nose, and mouth. The award-winning game's creators call Ned's Head "a wacky, silly, icky, sticky, and fun gross-out game." It is.

SECRET AGENT DOLL

The National Security Agency banned Furbys from their headquarters because these fuzzy toys have embedded computer chips that allow them to record and repeat what they "hear." Officials were afraid they might remember phrases that are **TOP SECRET**.

FEAR FACTOR

Check out these famous fraidy cats.

QUEEN ELIZABETH I. England's most famous queen had a fear of roses.

THOMAS EDISON. The inventor of the lightbulb was afraid of the dark.

ELVIS PRESLEY. As a young boy, the "king of rock 'n' roll" carried his own fork and knife to school. Why? His mother thought germs on the cafeteria's silverware would make him sick.

NIKOLA TESLA. One of the world's greatest inventors was deathly afraid of round objects—especially pearl necklaces.

MOZART. When he was little, this famous composer was so scared of trumpets that he would get physically ill when he heard one blow.

RAY BRADBURY. He writes of traveling to distant planets, but this famous sci-fi author is actually afraid to fly.

YOU'RE MY INSPIRATION

Strange beginnings for strange characters.

OSCAR THE GROUCH

Muppets creator Jim Henson and *Sesame Street* director Jon Stone always had lunch at a New York restaurant called Oscar's Tavern. Their waiter was the rudest, grouchiest man they'd ever met. But they thought he was funny… so funny that they used him as the model for Oscar, the world's most famous grouch.

COUNT DRACULA

The inspiration for this batty villain was Prince Vlad, a 15th century Romanian ruler who had a nasty habit of impaling his enemies on sharp stakes (and dipping his bread in their blood). Vlad the Impaler, as he was known to his enemies, was also called Dracula, or "son of the dragon."

FREDDY KRUEGER

Writer/director Wes Craven based the evil character in his *Nightmare on Elm Street* films after a kid named Freddy who harassed and bullied him in high school.

REVOLTING RECORDS

FARTHEST NOSE BLOW
On August 13, 1999, Scot Jeckel launched a marshmallow from his nostril into the mouth of his friend Ray Perisin. The record blow: a mighty 16 feet, $3\frac{1}{2}$ inches.

MOST COBRA KISSES
In 1999 Gordon Cates of Alachua, Florida, set a world record by kissing 11 deadly cobras in a row.

LOUDEST BURP
On April 5, 2000, Paul Hunn of London, England, burped one that registered 118.1 decibels. (That's almost as loud as a jumbo jet taking off.)

BIGGEST EYEBALL POPPER
Kim Goodman of Chicago set a strange world record on June 13, 1998, when she popped her eyeballs 11 millimeters (almost $\frac{1}{2}$-inch) out of their sockets.

FARTHEST CRICKET SPITTER
The world record for farthest dead cricket spitting is 32 feet. It was set in 1998 by Dan Capps at Purdue University's annual Bug Bowl in West Lafayette, Indiana.

FASTEST WORM EATER

On November 15, 2003, "Snake" Manoharan of Madras, India, ate 200 earthworms in 30 seconds, breaking the previous record set by American Mike Hogg. (Snake likes to finish off his worm-eating act by putting his pet snake up his nose and pulling it out through his mouth.)

FARTHEST MILK SQUIRT

Ilker Yilmaz has an unusual talent. He can squirt milk from his eye. And he squirts it farther than anyone else in the world. He proved it on September 1, 2004, when he shot some milk 9 feet 2 inches at the Armada Hotel in Istanbul, Turkey.

MOST TIME SPENT WITH SCORPIONS

Nur Malena Hassan from Malaysia set a world record in 2004. Her feat: she endured 36 days locked in a small glass box with 6,069 scorpions. The 27-year-old Scorpion Queen was stung 17 times…and lived to tell about it!

CREEPY CURES

Don't try these at home, but before modern medicine, people relied on folk remedies. How, for example, would they cure...

A TOOTHACHE?
Chew on a peppercorn.

SWOLLEN EYES?
Take a live crab; remove its eyes. Put the crab back in the water and put the eyeballs on your neck.

SORE THROAT?
Tie nine knots in a black thread and wear it around your neck for nine days.

SNAKEBITE?
Put earwax on the bite and ask someone to say a prayer for you.

INGROWN TOE-NAIL?
Using a leather string, tie a lizard's liver to your left ankle. The ingrown nail should disappear in nine days.

SHORTNESS OF BREATH?
Take the lungs and liver from a fox. Chop them up into tiny pieces, mix with wine, and drink the concoction from a church bell.

BURNS?
Mix sheep dung with fresh goose grease and spread it on the affected area.

FRECKLES?
Four-day-old lemon juice rubbed on the face will make them go away.

CUTS?
Apply a large army ant to the cut, so that it takes hold of each side of the wound with its pincers. Cut the body off, leaving the ant's head to hold the cut together.

CAT MAN DO

Dennis Avner, 48, is a computer programmer by day…but a tiger by night (and day). Tattooed from head to toe in orange and black stripes, he has filed his teeth to make them look like cat fangs and keeps his fingernails talon-sharp. He's had plastic surgery to give his lips a permanent snarl and had latex whiskers implanted under his nose. And if that's not enough, Avner, who goes by his American Indian name, Stalking Cat, plans to have real tiger fur grafted onto his skin like a permanent wig. "When I have the coat of a tiger," says Avner, "I feel I will have reached my goal in life."

BODY BY YOU

Your tears are made of the same ingredients as your pee.

Your head weighs about as much as a lightweight bowling ball.

Ear wax naturally dries up and forms into little balls, which fall out when you eat and sleep.

Your eye gook is made of the same stuff as your boogers. (Yuck!)

Your armpits are *supposed* to sweat. That's how they get rid of the poisons in your body.

Your mouth will make 25,000 quarts of spit in your lifetime—enough to fill two swimming pools.

Your stomach acid can dissolve razor blades.

Your fingers have no muscles—only tendons that are powered by your arm muscles.

Your entire skeleton is replaced cell by cell every seven years.

You fart about 14 times every day.

Each foot has 250,000 sweat glands, which produce up to a pint of sweat per day.

Your body's largest organ: your skin

Your toenails have traces of gold in them.

EW! GROSS!

BOMBS AWAY!

Joe Carlone and his wife spent 12 years trying to rid their house of a terrible smell, but nothing seemed to help. Then one day their kitchen wall burst and 40 gallons of sewage gushed into the room. Years before, a telephone installer had accidentally punctured a pipe coming from the upstairs bathroom. The walls became so packed with poop they exploded.

NAVEL JELLY

Most people wash out their belly button lint, but not Graham Barker. He's been collecting his for more than 20 years, earning him a Guinness world record: "Most Belly Button Lint." When he gets enough fluff, he plans on stuffing a pillow with it.

WHO DEALT IT SMELT IT

What is the world's stinkiest substance? It's a tie between "The U.S. Government Standard Bathroom Malodor" and "Who Me?" Both are used by the military in stink bombs, as a way to break up riots. One reeks of rotting food and sulfur; the other smells like human poop.

THE MOST HAUNTED HOUSE IN ENGLAND

More than a dozen ghosts wander the halls and grounds of this old mansion!

Littledean Hall in Gloucestershire is the oldest continuously occupied home in England. Built in the 5th century on a sacred Celtic site, this ancient manor is said to be home to no fewer than 16 ghosts.

Visitors find themselves shoved, jerked, and punched by unseen hands. They also report smells of rotting flesh, burned toast, and roses. (It's no wonder guests have suffered

attacks of dizziness, nausea, and heart palpitations.)

WHERE TO FIND THE GHOSTS

• Visitors coming up the drive may be greeted by a

phantom gardener who resembles one of the previous lords of the manor.

• The ghost of a servant who murdered his master wanders the halls between his bedroom and the drawing room, wearing a silver collar and carrying a lit candle.

• The ghosts of Captain Wigmore and Colonel Congrove, both of whom died gruesome deaths, still haunt the dining room. Blood stains often appear on the wood floors and are quickly scrubbed away…only to return.

• A ghostly monk walks from the dining room into a secret passage in the library leading down to the cellar and underground to the nearby grange of Flaxley Abbey.

• In the Blue Bedroom, swords clash and pistol shots ring out as two brothers duel eternally over a lady love.

WEIRD UNDERWEAR

Boxers, briefs...or these?

INFLATABLE UNDERPANTS

Katsuo Katugoru of Tokyo, Japan, was so afraid of drowning that he invented something to protect him in case of emergency: inflatable underpants. Unfortunately, his underwear accidentally inflated while he was on the subway, instantly expanding to 30 times their normal size and nearly suffocating his seatmates. Luckily, some quick-thinking passengers burst his bubble—saving the day by stabbing the undies with pens and pencils.

WOLF MAN

Only 50 cases of this rare genetic condition have been documented since the Middle Ages. Could it be the root of wolf man legends around the world?

J esus Fajardo Aceves is truly one-of-a-kind. Or rather, one-of-a-family. Twenty-four members of the Aceves family in Zacatecas, Mexico, have *hypertrichosis*, a genetic disorder that makes hair grow all over a person's body, including his face.

Very little is known about the condition because it shows up in only one out of ten billion people. Some scientists believe "the curse of the hair" is caused by a holdover gene from the distant past, when humans were as hairy as apes.

What we do know is that throughout history, people with hypertrichosis have suffered terribly. They've been treated as freaks, put on display in circuses, or even worse, feared as monsters. But the truth is that "wolf people," as the Aceves family proudly call themselves, are completely normal...except for their hair!

☆ WHIZ KIDS ☆

☆ *Here are three stories of uniquely gifted kids.*

MICHAEL KEARNEY (b. 1984) started talking when he was four months old. Two months later, baby Michael surprised his family again. He wasn't feeling well, so his mother took him to the doctor. That's when he told the doctor, "I have a left ear infection." When Michael was ten months old, his dad asked his mom, "Why don't we go out and get some F-R-E-N-C-H F-R-I-E-S?" "That sounds good," Michael piped up. "Let's go to M-C-D-O-N-A-L-D-S."

Michael entered high school at the age of five and finished nine months later. He was 10 when he graduated from college, and broke a Guinness world record at 14 by graduating from Middle Tennessee State University with a masters degree in chemistry.

JAY GREENBERG (b. 1991) likes to be called Blue Jay because, like Jay, a blue jay is small and makes lots of noise. But Jay doesn't exactly make noise—he composes orchestral music.

At two years old Jay started drawing musical instruments. One day he drew a cello and told his parents he wanted one. When his mother finally took him to a music store, Jay sat down at a miniature cello and immediately began to play, beautifully.

Jay started composing music the following year, when he was just three. Jay uses a computer program to write music, sometimes writing so fast that his computer crashes. In a field where talented composers might write five or six symphonies in their entire lifetime, Jay already composed five symphonies… before the age of 13.

GREGORY R. SMITH (b. 1989) learned how to read when he was two years old. He became a vegetarian that same year when he noticed that humans, like the herbivore dinosaurs he was studying, have flat teeth. Greg graduated from high school at 10 and earned a college degree in mathematics when he was 13.

He now works promoting nonviolence and world peace through the organization he founded, International Youth Advocates. And he's been nominated for the Nobel Peace Prize three times (he was just 12 years old when he was first nominated).

DOUBLE TROUBLE

Are twins more connected than normal siblings?

OH, BROTHER!

Identical twins from Piqua, Ohio, were adopted by families from different towns. The twins met again at age 39 and discovered

some remarkable facts: Both were named James. Each had married and divorced a woman named Linda, then married a woman named Betty. One's son was named James Alan; the other's was James Allen. Both did well in math and liked woodworking and drove the same model car and both had dogs named Toy. The biggest difference? James Lewis had short hair combed back; James Springer had long hair combed forward.

OH, SISTER!

In 1948 Diane Lamb broke two ribs in a train crash. At that exact moment her twin sister, who lived in another town, felt a stabbing pain in her chest, fell out of her chair, and broke the same two ribs.

OUCH! OUCH!

Roberto and Marco were identical twins who made a parachute jump together near Milan, Italy. Roberto broke his leg on landing. Two hours later Marco crashed his car while driving home…and broke *his* leg.

LUCKY FINDS #1

*Keep your eyes open—you never know
when luck might be on your side.*

THE FIND: A diamond

WHERE: Under a yam

THE STORY: In 1997 three orphan boys from Sierra Leone, Africa, were scrounging for food. They had already gone hungry for two days when, after a luckless morning of searching for yams near the village of Hinnah Malen, the starving boys gave up and decided to walk home. While walking along the road, they spotted a yam under a palm tree. As the boys pried the yam out of the ground, they discovered a flawless 100-carat diamond worth half a million dollars.

"86 THE BUNPUPS"

That's restaurant lingo for, "We're out of hot dogs." Here are some more:

"ADAM AND EVE ON A RAFT"
Two poached eggs on toast

"AN M.D."
A Dr Pepper

"BOSSY IN A BOWL"
Beef stew

"WAX"
American cheese

"HOUSE-BOAT"
A banana split

"MIKE AND IKE"
Salt and pepper shakers

"PUT A HAT ON IT"
Add ice cream

"LIFE PRESERVERS"
Doughnuts

"COW PASTE"
Butter

"NERVOUS PUDDING"
Jell-o

"PAINT A BOW-WOW RED"
A hot dog with ketchup

"HOLD THE HAIL"
No ice

"THROW IT IN THE MUD"
Add chocolate syrup

LOST AND FOUND

There are no "finders keepers, losers weepers" here.

LOST: A bus ticket

FOUND: Jack Crackers of Derbyshire, England, lost a bus ticket when he was just a teenager. Years later, at age 75, he was slapped on the back during a coughing fit and it fell out of his ear. Crackers got his ticket back and also his hearing— he'd been deaf in that ear for 60 years!

LOST: A wedding ring

FOUND: Mrs. Gudebrod of California lost her wedding ring during a picnic at a beach. A year later her husband brought home a crab he'd caught on the same beach. Guess what they found stuck to one of the crab's claws? Mrs. G's wedding ring.

WARNING!

Ever been warned not to do something stupid—so stupid that you would never even consider doing it? Here are some real labels found on real products.

On a Batman costume
"WARNING: CAPE DOES NOT ENABLE USER TO FLY."

On a toilet brush
"CAUTION: DO NOT USE FOR PERSONAL HYGIENE."

On a household iron
"WARNING: NEVER IRON CLOTHES WHILE THEY ARE BEING WORN."

On a washing machine
"CAUTION: YOU MUST REMOVE CLOTHES BEFORE WASHING"

On a king-size mattress
"WARNING: DO NOT ATTEMPT TO SWALLOW."

NATURE IS STRANGE

Weird facts from the natural world.

- Elephants are the only mammals that can't jump.

- Hummingbirds can't walk.

- Bees kill more people than snakes do.

- A rat can go longer without water than a camel.

- Possums don't actually "play" dead. They pass out from fear...and *look* dead.

- Only the female mosquito bites.

- A pregnant goldfish is called a *twit*.

- Crickets hear through their knees; butterflies taste with their feet.

- Snakes can see through their eyelids.

- Kangaroos can't jump backward.

- Mosquitoes prefer children to adults and blondes to brunettes.

- The venom of a female black widow spider is more potent than that of a rattlesnake.

- The praying mantis is the only insect that can rotate its head 360 degrees.

- More than 10,000 birds a year die from smashing into windows!

KING TUT'S CURSE

Who believes in curses? We do.

On November 26, 1922, a team led by a British archaeologist named Howard Carter entered the ancient Egyptian tomb of King Tutankhamen. Within seven years of that date, 11 of the 13 Europeans who were present when the tomb was opened were dead. Some believe a fungus found growing on the tomb's walls killed the explorers. Others believe the tomb was cursed.

What do *you* think?

THE FACTS

 On the day King Tut's tomb was opened, a vulture circled overhead. The archaeologists thought this was particularly strange. Why? Because according to legend, the tomb was guarded by Nekhbet, the vulture goddess. Her curse was printed above the door.

 Three months later, Lord Carnarvon, who had financed the expedition, was the first to go. He died crying, "There's a bird…scratching my face!" At the exact moment he passed away, the lights went out in Cairo and his dog at home in England howled in anguish…and then dropped dead.

 That same year Richard Bethell, Howard Carter's secretary, died of heart failure.

 A short time later, Arthur Mace, one of the archaeologists in the group who opened the tomb, fell into a coma. He died in 1923.

Hugh Evelyn-White, another archaeologist with the expedition, hung himself in 1924. He left a note that read: "I have succumbed to a curse which forces me to disappear."

The year the tomb was opened, a worker stole a piece of King Tut's jewelry. A relative of the thief returned it to the authorities 83 years later. Why? The curse. From the time the relative received the jewel, four untimely deaths had struck her family.

HOW TO MAKE A MUMMY

An ancient secret recipe.

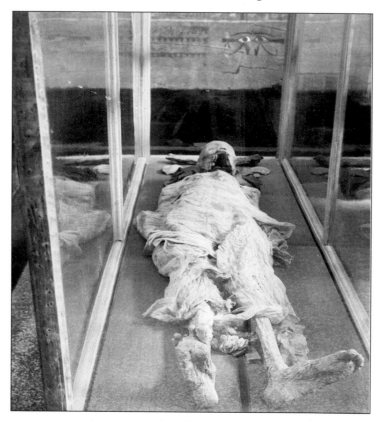

┌───┐

INGREDIENTS:

- 1 dead body
- 1 crochet hook
- several jars
- 400 pounds of salt

- frankincense
- myrrh
- lots of linen
- a small amulet

└───┘

STEP ONE:

1. Using the crochet hook, pull the brains out through the nose.

2. Make a small incision in the belly and take out everything except the heart.

3. Place all the entrails (the stuff you pulled out) in the jars.

4. Stuff packets of salt inside the body, then completely cover the outside of the body with the rest of the salt.

5. Wait at least 35 days for the body to dry out and become mummified.

STEP TWO:

1. Carefully remove the salt.

2. Gently anoint the body with frankincense and myrrh (two ancient types of fragrant tree resin).

3. Wrap the body in layer after layer of linen strips.

4. During the wrapping procedure, place the small amulet over the heart. Decorate each layer with hiero-glyphic prayers.

STEP THREE:

For the total effect, let mummy rest undisturbed for at least a thousand years.

SLEEPING BEAUTY
The true tale of a real-life Rip Van Winkle.

On February 3, 1866, Mollie Fancher, a 23-year-old Brooklyn woman, felt dizzy and collapsed on the floor in a faint. Her aunt put her to bed, thinking Mollie would come out of it. But she didn't.

For the next 46 years, Mollie lay in a trance, barely breathing, eating, or drinking. Doctors were baffled. None knew what had caused this strange sleep, nor what to do about it. Then, nine years into her trance-like state, Mollie began to display amazing powers. She could describe the dress and actions of people hundreds of miles away, and could read unopened letters.

One famous test of her powers involved sealing a secret message inside three envelopes and then hiding it in her doctor's office five miles away. When the doctor asked Mollie what was in the envelope, she whispered, "Written on a sheet of paper are the words, 'Lincoln was shot by a crazed actor.'" She was right.

Mollie Fancher became known as the "Brooklyn Enigma" (an enigma is something mysterious and hard to understand). Then one day in 1912, the 70-year-old woman woke up. She lived three more years, but she remains an enigma. To this day, no one has ever fully explained what caused her long, strange sleep.

NEVERMORE

Every year on the nineteenth of January, a mysterious man sneaks into a locked graveyard in Baltimore, Maryland, and places three roses and a half-empty bottle of cognac on Edgar Allan Poe's grave. Poe, author of dark poems and stories like "The Raven" and "The Telltale Heart," died in 1849.

Jeff Jerome, curator of the Poe House and Museum, says the man first appeared in 1949. In 1993 the mystery mourner, who always wore a scarf and black hat, left a note that read, "The torch will be passed."

In 1999, the fifty-first year, a new mourner appeared. This one followed the same ritual as the previous mystery man, placing the roses and cognac bottle on Poe's grave. He put his hand on top of the tombstone and bowed his head for five minutes. And then he disappeared... into the fog.

SPOOKY SPOTS

Want to see a ghost? Visit scary Olde England—
there are plenty of ghosts for everyone.

BORLEY RECTORY IN ESSEX

According to local legend, in the 17th century, a woman named Marie Laire was strangled by her husband and buried in the cellar of a monastery. Two hundred years later, Reverend Henry Bull unknowingly built Borley Rectory on the site where the monastery once stood. Marie Laire soon made her presence known. She often appeared at Reverend Bull's window, staring at him with vacant eyes. Bull was so upset that he bricked up the window... but the ghostly legend grew:

• In 1923, new owners called in a psychic investigator, who witnessed vases flying into walls, keys leaping from their keyholes, and messages being tapped out on a mirror.

• When the Reverend Lionel Foyster moved into the rectory, messages began to appear on the walls asking Foyster's wife, Marianne, to "please get help."

• In 1939 a mysterious fire destroyed the house. Some local residents claimed to have seen a nun at an upper window peering out over the flames.

THE INDUSTRIAL MUSEUM IN DERBY. Built on the site of an old silk mill, the museum's tower is haunted by the ghost of a little boy who worked at the factory and died when he was kicked down the stairs by one of the bosses. The staff often hear crying and run into the tower thinking there's a lost child inside. But it's always empty. Instead they find the elevator going up and down... by itself.

THE THEATRE ROYAL AT MARGATE. This theater doesn't need to put on scary shows—it's scary enough as it is. Many actors say they've heard a scream and seen an orange ball of light traveling across the stage before exiting through the stage door. An apparition sometimes appears in a box in the balcony and draws back the curtains if they are closed.

THE CROWN HOTEL IN YORKSHIRE. This 17th-century inn is now a three-star hotel that hosts a number of ghostly guests. The most famous: a waitress who was murdered by the chef and now wanders the corridors crying. A lady in a gown has been spotted in the lobby, where temperatures suddenly drop dramatically. One permanent resident of the hotel is often awakened by the ghost of a little girl sitting on her bed, and the ghost of the notorious highway robber Dick Turpin is heard galloping by outside.

TOMBSTONE TALES

If you're ever in Ohio, stop by and say AHHH!

GREAT BALL OF MYSTERY

Marion Cemetery in Marion, Ohio, is home to the "Merchant Ball." This 5,200-pound granite ball—the gravestone for the Charles Merchant family—rests solidly on a stone pedestal, but ever since 1898 it has rotated...all by itself. The family first noticed the phenomenon when a spot where the granite had not been polished suddenly

appeared. They tried to stop the ball from spinning. They had a crane lift the 2½-ton stone and tar it back into place. But it continued to turn!

What causes the mystery movement? Some say a restless spirit moves the ball. Others think it's a result of temperature changes, which make the base expand and contract. But that would leave scratches in the ball—there aren't any. It seems to float on its pedestal.

There are other stone balls in the Marion Cemetery, but they don't turn. The Merchant Ball remains an unsolved mystery.

ASHES TO ASHES?

Not everyone wants to end up six feet under. Edward Headrick, who invented the Frisbee, wanted his ashes molded into a Frisbee and tossed around. Here are some more ash-tonishing endings.

ASHES TO DIAMONDS. LifeGem Memorials turns dead people's remains into diamonds. The concept is simple. Humans and diamonds are both made up of carbon. Add pressure and heat and you've got a gem that will last forever. What's more, the average person's ashes contain enough carbon to make 50 to 100 beautiful diamonds.

ASHES TO ART. Wayne Gilbert, an artist from Texas, has made the amazing (and gruesome) discovery that every person has a unique color—even after death. He found this out when he mixed a person's ashes with resin…and color suddenly appeared. Now he turns people into paintings.

ASHES TO REEFS. Want to spend eternity with fish? Eternal Reefs mixes the ashes of deceased  people with cement to create balls that are dropped into the ocean to create artificial reefs. The fish love the reefs.

ASHES TO SPACE DUST. A company called Celestis will launch the ashes of your loved one into deep space. "Families can look up into the night sky and know their loved ones are up there somewhere."

GHOST HUNTER

Who you gonna call? Nancy, of course.

In the 1970s, Professor Nancy Acuff was driving home from her job at East Tennessee University when she hit what she later called a "time warp." Suddenly she was transported back in time to the 1800s. Her home was gone and in its place stood a log cabin. She watched a man on horseback gallop up to the cabin door and yell for someone to come out. When a young boy appeared, the rider whirled around and galloped back down the road. Then, just as suddenly, everything changed back to the 1970s.

When a similar incident occurred a year later, Acuff did some investigating and concluded that the "man" was her home's previous owner, Jacob Storm, the first mayor of Blountville, Tennessee. Word of Professor Acuff's ghost hunting spread and soon she was getting calls from people with haunted homes of their own.

Acuff believes there is a difference between spirits and ghosts. Ghosts always do the same thing at the same location, but spirits are generally the souls of dead relatives who have some message or warning they want to impart. And Professor Acuff is there to receive it.

BAD GHOSTS!

Go on, spend the night here—we dare you.

The Ancient Ram Inn is an 800-year-old inn built on a pagan burial site in England. What scares most visitors is the creepy feeling that the spirits here are not friendly. John Humphries, who has lived there for 30 years, says he has been pushed against walls, knocked over, and had his bed shaken. Once he even felt something clawing at his bed like an animal.

But it is the Bishop's Room that frightens most people away. According to Julie Hunt, a well-known ghost hunter, the room is home to five phantoms, including a cavalier, a monk, and a witch.

In 1999 she took this photograph of a blurry figure in the room, which she believes is conclusive evidence of ghostly activity in the Ancient Ram Inn.

TA MOKO

The Maoris—the native people of New Zealand—were legendary warriors of the South Pacific. Ta moko is Maori for "to be tattooed." They awed their enemies with their amazing tattoos.

WHO GOT TA MOKO

All high-ranking Maori were tattooed as a rite of passage into adulthood. When young men and women reached age 12 or 13, girls tattooed their chins and boys got a full-face tattoo. The tattoos told not only a person's social status but also what tribe and clan he came from—even what he did for a living. The designs were so unique that during the 18th century, Maori men would sign legal documents by pressing their faces against the paper like a signature. Most young Maoris tattooed only their faces but they often added tattoos to

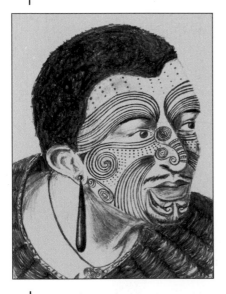

other parts of their bodies to mark important events in their lives. North Auckland warriors were famous for the double spirals tattooed from their butts to their knees. *Ta moko* was an incredibly painful ordeal that could last for days. But everyone tried to get through it. Why? Because not to have moko made you a real loser in Maori society.

HOW *TA MOKO* WAS DONE

The ta moko artist would study a young Maori's face for hours, even days, working out a design. Then he carved deep cuts into the skin with a bone chisel. Only the Maori did tattoos in this way (other Polynesians like the Samoans and Hawaiians used needles, which is the way most tattoos are made today). Next he dipped the chisel into a mixture of burned *kauri* tree gum and caterpillars and tapped the sooty powder into the grooves in the skin.

"OW! THAT HURTS!"

The pain a young Maori endured was so intense that friends and relatives would play flutes and chant poems to keep his mind off it. Sometimes the Maori would pass out or, even worse, quit, which shamed him for life. But getting the tattoo was just the first part of the ordeal. Once the tattoo artist was finished, leaves from the *karaka* tree were put on the cuts to help them heal, and that process took months. Nothing was allowed to touch the swollen wounds, which could get infected, so the Maori was fed liquid food and water through a wooden funnel. Depending on where the tattoos had been placed, he might not be able to get up and move around. But six months later the young Maori was usually fit enough to walk proudly out among his or her people with a totally new look.

THE AMITYVILLE HORROR

This story was the subject of a best-selling book and a very creepy movie. Is it truth...or fiction?

On November 13, 1974, six members of the DeFeo family were murdered by their oldest son, Ronald, in their home in Amityville, New York. One year later, George and Cathy Lutz and their three children moved into that home. Twenty-eight days later, the Lutz family moved out. Here are the reasons why.

Black goo oozed out of keyholes in the doors.

Father Ray Pecoraro was brought in to bless the house. When he did, he felt an unseen hand slap him and heard a voice say, "Get out."

Terrible odors filled the house.

The family heard weird music, like a brass band tuning up before playing.

The Lutz family heard thumping and scratching sounds.

Locked windows and doors opened and closed on their own.

Swarms of houseflies mysteriously appeared.

A devil-like creature was seen outside the window at night.

The temperature in the house would go from hot to freezing cold.

The toilet water turned black.

Household objects moved about on their own.

Green slime oozed out of the walls and ceiling.

HOW TO READ TEA LEAVES

Learn the ancient Chinese art of tasseography and unlock the secrets of your future.

SUPPLIES

• A plain, light colored tea cup and saucer. Make sure the cup has a wide opening and narrow base.

• A teaspoon of loose tea

• Hot water

INSTRUCTIONS

1. Put the loose tea in an empty cup. (If you have only tea bags, cut open two bags and pour the contents into the cup.)

2. Fill cup with hot water. Let the tea steep for a few minutes.

3. Sip the tea. While you're drinking, think of a question.

4. Stop drinking before you get to the last few drops of tea. There should be one or two teaspoons of liquid and the tea leaves at the bottom of cup.

5. Swirl the cup counterclockwise three times with your left hand (or right hand if you're left-handed).

6. Immediately after swirling, turn the cup over onto the saucer. Drain the liquid. Then turn the cup over with the handle pointing toward you.

READING THE TEA LEAVES:

1. The handle is Home. Anything you see here is bound to strike close to home.

2. The rim is the Present.

3. The walls are the Immediate Future.

4. The bottom is the Distant Future.

Reading tea leaves is like seeing shapes in the clouds. Use the guide below to interpret the shapes. Start at the handle and work your way down to the bottom.

TASSEOGRAPHY "SYMBOLS"

Elephant: Wisdom

Bird: Good news

Mountain: An obstacle or challenge

Sun: Joy and power

Moon: Fame and riches

Airplane or train: Travel

Eyeglasses: Study the situation thoroughly

Octopus: Overwhelming; too much to do

Fish: Good news from far away

Heart: Love

Cat: Treachery

Key: Problem solved

Knot: An argument

Lock: Something to be solved or opened

Volcano: A situation about to erupt

Coins: Prosperity

Mouse: Thief nearby

Letters: First letter of someone's name

Spider: Unexpected inheritance

Dog: Faithful friend

Clouds: Wishes coming true

Teardrop: Disappointment or sadness

WILL POWER

People have left some pretty strange requests in their wills.

HAPPY BIRTHDAY TO YOU

Robert Louis Stevenson, the author of *Treasure Island*, left his birthday to a good friend who had always complained about being born on Christmas.

A CLASS ACT

Edwin Forrest was a leading stage actor in the 1800s who left all his money to the Actors Fund to establish a retirement home for his fellow actors. But he had two conditions: 1) They had to do a reading of Shakespeare on Shakespeare's birthday; and 2) The Declaration of Independence had to be read every 4th of July.

TAKE THAT!

An Australian named Lord Francis Reginal left one shilling to his wife "for tram fare so she can go somewhere and drown herself."

NO MONKEYING AROUND

Patricia O'Neill got angry at her husband and left her estate to her chimp, Kalu. The ape's take: $100 million!

MONEY FOR HER MAKER

A woman in Cherokee County, North Carolina, left her entire estate to God. The court told the county sheriff to try to find the beneficiary. A few days later the sheriff returned and submitted this report: "After due and diligent search, God cannot be found in this county."

HIGHWAY TO HEAVEN

Sandra West was a wealthy socialite from Beverly Hills who left her brother $3 million, provided that he buried her in her lace nightgown and sitting in her Ferrari, with the seat at a comfortable slant. So that's what he did—but then he poured concrete over the Ferrari so no one would be tempted to dig her up and drive the car away.

BIG AND SMALL

The world's longest will was 95,000 words long. The tiniest will was written on the back of a postage stamp.

PUSHING UP DAISIES

These are from real gravestones—really!

Here lies
Ann Mann,

Who lived
an old maid

But died an
old Mann.

Here lies
the body of
Jonathan Blake

Stepped
on the gas

Instead of the brake.

Here lies
Lester Moore
Four slugs
from a .44
No Les
No More.

Stranger,

Tread this ground
with gravity;

Dentist Brown
is filling

His last cavity.

THE HAUNTED PAINTING

O n February 2, 2000, a California couple put a very strange item up for sale on eBay: a haunted painting. An art dealer originally found the painting behind an abandoned brewery and sold it to them. They hung the 24- by 36-inch painting in their living room…and

that's when the trouble began. One morning their four-year-old daughter announced that the "children in the picture were fighting." The couple claimed to have caught the ghosts in the painting in action with a motion-triggered camera. And now they wanted to get rid of it.

As word of the auction spread across the Web, more than 13,000 people viewed the painting. Some people swore that looking at it made them physically ill, as if they were possessed by an evil spirit. No one knows what the family originally paid for the picture, but they sold it for $1,025.

GOT GHOSTS?

Think there may be ghosts in your house?
Here's how experts say you can tell.

TEN TELLTALE SIGNS THAT YOUR HOUSE IS HAUNTED

• You feel a cool breeze even though the windows are closed.

• You hear voices that come from nowhere and you feel like someone is watching you.

• You hear footsteps walking in and out of empty rooms.

• You smell roses, oranges, or an "electric" odor.

• Jewelry, shoes, tools, and other small items are moved from one location to another... but nobody (nobody human, that is) moved them.

• Lights and electrical appliances turn on and off by themselves.

• Your bedcovers are thrown off you.

• You feel a warm touch on your back or shoulders. (The touch of a ghost is always warm, never cold.)

• You receive repeat phone calls from a caller who never identifies himself.

• You see flashes of light or movement out of the corner of your eye, yet when you look there's nothing there.

GHOSTBUSTING TIPS

Okay, so you know you've got ghosts. Now what do you do? Here are five tips.

1. TALK TO THE GHOST. Let him know that this is your house and he must stop bothering you or leave immediately. Shout if you must.

2. SHOE SHUFFLE. Put your shoes at the foot of your bed, with one shoe pointing one way and the other pointing in the opposite direction. This confuses the ghosts and they leave.

3. GET THE DIRT. Take a scoop of dirt from the path to your front door and dump it in a nearby grave-yard. The ghosts will follow.

4. PAINT YOUR FRONT DOOR RED. Ghosts won't enter a home with a red door.

5. GET OUT THE VACUUM. If all else fails, clean your house. Ghosts don't like clean homes.

SOLD!

Surfing the Internet? Some pretty strange things are being sold on eBay.

ITEM: A ghost and his former cane.

STORY: Mary Anderson placed her father's "ghost" up for auction when her son, Collin, told her that his grandpa had come back to haunt him. She had only one request for the winning bidder: "I would like you to write a letter after you've received the cane (and the ghost) to my son, letting him know that his grandfather is there with you and you're getting along great."

SOLD: $65,000

ITEM: Grilled cheese sandwich.

STORY: This sandwich was saved in a refrigerator for ten years because it appeared to bear the image of the Virgin Mary.

SOLD: $28,000

ITEM: Leftover french toast

STORY: It's Justin Timberlake's partially eaten french toast (with extra syrup) plus the fork and plate he used when he was appearing on the Z100 morning radio show.

SOLD: $3,154

ITEM: "Stuff Found in Couch"

STORY: Found while looking for TV remote: three pieces of Big Red chewing gum, a screw, 80¢, two rubber bands, a peppermint candy, a paper clip, a red cap from a Bic pen, a wrapper from a Starburst candy, a partial box of matches, the edge of a piece of paper from a spiral bound notebook, a few shards from a pecan shell, and a third of a pretzel.

SOLD: $3.06 (plus $3.20 shipping)

ITEM: A piece of Nutri-Grain cereal with the image of E.T.

STORY: The E.T. grain was rescued from a bowl of cereal seconds before the milk was poured on it.

SOLD: $1,035

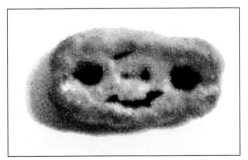

HIDE AND SEEK?

World War II ended in 1945...but
somebody forgot to tell this guy.

Lieutenant Hiroo Onoda of the Imperial Japanese Army survived in the jungles of the tiny Philippine island of Lubang for nearly three decades by hunting in the forests and stealing food from villagers. Then on February 20, 1974, Onoda met a young Japanese adventurer named Norio Suzuki, who had come to the Philippines to search for him. The two became friends, and Suzuki explained to the old warrior that the fighting had stopped a long time ago. Yet when he asked Onoda to return to Japan, Onoda said he would not leave his post without direct orders from one of his commanders. On March 9, 1974, Norio Suzuki brought Onoda's onetime superior commander, Major Taniguchi, who delivered the orders for Onoda to surrender.

BIG DEAL

At 7 feet, 8.95 inches, Mongolian herdsman Xi Shun has won the title of World's Tallest Living Man from the previous world record holder, Radhouane Charbib of Tunisia, who is a mere 7 feet, 8.9 inches tall.

A-TISKET, A-TASKET

Some strange and scary caskets!

CAN YOU HEAR ME NOW? Want to talk to a deceased loved one but feel silly muttering at a mound of dirt? Now you can call directly into their casket with the new Telephonic Angel. The system has a loudspeaker that was designed by Juergen Broether as a way to talk to his mother who died in 1998.

PROFESSIONAL BOXERS. In Ghana, clients of Isaac Sowah and other fantasy coffin makers like to go out in style. Some choose a coffin that reflects their line of business: a shoemaker may want to be buried in a large shoe or a fisherman in a big fish. Others choose elephants, eagles, airplanes, or even mobile phones. Sowah says cars are very popular, especially Mercedes and Cadillacs.

DUMB CROOKS

These guys are one taco short of a "combo plate."

IT'S IN THE BAG...OR NOT

In Portland, Oregon, a man attempted to rob a bank by slipping a note to the teller. The note read: "This is a holdup, and I've got a gun. Put all the money in a paper bag." The teller refused to give him the money and wrote this note back to the man: "I don't have a paper bag."

GET A GRIP

If you're going to steal groceries there's one thing you should remember: don't stuff a lobster in your underwear. That's what Winston Treadway did, and was he sorry! He had already crammed a number of food items in his clothes and was sneaking toward the exit when a giant claw clamped down on his private parts. His cries of pain attracted the grocery clerks, who immediately called the police. The police arrested Winston, who was still in the lobster's grip. They finally had to use a set of pliers to pry open the angry lobster's claw.

RING-A-DING-DING

When a guy in Michigan tried to rob a Burger King, the clerk at the counter told him he couldn't open the cash register without a food order. So the would-be robber ordered onion rings. When the clerk told him that it was still breakfast time and onion rings were not yet available, the guy gave up and went home.

PICK ME!

When Los Angeles detectives asked each man in a police lineup to repeat the words, "Give me all your money or I'll shoot," the real robber shouted, "That's not what I said!" He was promptly thrown in jail.

FILL 'ER UP

When two gas station attendants in Iona, Michigan, refused to give a drunken robber any money, the drunk threatened to call the cops. They still refused, so the tipsy thief called the police, who came…and arrested him.

SIGN IN PLEASE

In 1987 five teenagers were arrested for spray painting graffiti all over the Lincoln Memorial in Washington, D.C. How did the police know who did it? The culprits spray painted their names on the monument.

e ALPHABET SOUP *g*

Ready for some wordplay? Letter rip!

• If the English alphabet was lined up in the order of most commonly used letters to the least used, it would look like this: E T A I S O N H R D L U C M F W Y P G V B K J Q X Z

• The first word spoken on the moon was "Okay."

• No word rhymes with *orange*, *purple*, or *month*.

• *Taphephobia* is the fear of being buried alive.

• Q is the only letter in the alphabet that doesn't appear in any of the names of the 50 United States.

• The most common name in the world: Muhammad.

• Smokey the Bear's original name was "Hot Foot Teddy."

• *Set* has more definitions than any other word.

• Compulsive nose picking is called *rhinotillexomania.*

• *Pants* was considered a dirty word in England in the 1880s.

• The world's longest place name is in New Zealand. *Taumatawhakatangihangakoauauotamateaturipukakapiki-maungahoronukupokaiwhenuakitanatahu* is Maori and means, "The brow of the hill where Tamatea—the man with the big knees who slid down, climbed up, and swallowed mountains, traveled the land and is known as the Land Eater—played his nose flute to his loved one."

WEIRD WORLD OF SPORTS

Beyond baseball, basketball, and football.

EXTREME CROQUET

It's more than just using mallets to hit balls through wickets—extreme croquet involves trees, cliffs, water hazards, mud, vines, and great distances. Started in the 1920s, a group of Swedish students perfected it in 1975. Now it has mallets that look more like sledgehammers, two-story-tall wickets, and balls that are able to withstand a good strong *thwack* in the deep, dark woods. (Cheating is encouraged.)

SHIN KICKING

Also known as "purring" in Wales, here's how it's played: Two men stand face to face with their hands on each other's shoulders. They wear reinforced shoes. At the signal, they start kicking each other's shins until one loses his grip on his opponent. (This sport has failed to catch on in other nations.)

TOE WRESTLING

The World Championships are held each year in a pub in Wetton, England. The contestants sit on the floor with their right foot down and left foot in the air. They lock toes and attempt to press their opponent's foot to the floor. (If a player is in too much pain, he is allowed to stop the proceedings by yelling "Toe much!")

WIFE CARRYING

It's the extreme sport of choice in Finland.
A man carries his wife over a 780-foot course,
through water, sand, and grass and
over fences. Dropping your wife
results in a 15-second
penalty. The prize?
The wife's weight
in lemonade.

AMAZING COINCIDENCES

Strange things are happening!

LUCK OF THE IRISH. For years, Mrs. Coyle of Glasgow, Scotland, carried a lucky sixpence with her initials on it. The day before she went to Ireland she accidentally spent it. She was heartbroken...until two days later when, while shopping in a small Irish village, the coin with her initials was given back to her in change.

LOTS OF STOTTS. In 1985 John Stott crashed his car. The accident was witnessed by Bernard Stott. The investigator on the scene was Tina Stott. All three Stotts went to the police station where they met desk sergeant Walter Stott. None of the Stotts were related.

BETTER LATE THAN DEAD. On March 1, 1950, a church choir in Beatrice, Nebraska, cheated death by an amazing stroke of luck. The 15 singers met at the same time every week for practice—7:15 p.m.—but that night everyone was late. One had car trouble, another wanted to hear the end of a radio show, another had to finish some chores at home. That's why no one was inside the church when a gas leak caused an explosion at 7:25.

HAIL TO THE CHIEFS. Three of the first five presidents of the United States—John Adams, Thomas Jefferson, and James Monroe—all died on the same day of the year: July 4th.

THE TRAVELING PANTS

The gift that kept on giving.

L arry Kunkel didn't like the pants his mother gave him for Christmas in 1964. So the next Christmas, Kunkel wrapped them and gave them to his brother-in-law, Roy Collette. But Collette didn't want them either. So he gave the pants back to Kunkel the following year. The men continued this friendly back and forth gift exchange for the next 10 years…and then the rules changed.

In 1974 Collette stuffed the pants into a three-foot-long, one-inch pipe, and gave the pipe to Kunkel, who accepted the challenge. The two men traded the pants back and forth for another 15 years, each time finding more clever ways to deliver them. They were delivered in a four-ton concrete Rubik's Cube, locked inside a 600-pound safe, cemented into a monster tire, and put in the backseat of a car that was then crushed into a three-foot cube.

There was only one rule to Collette and Kunkel's gift exchange: if the pants were damaged, the game would stop. In 1989 the pants caught fire and burned when Collette tried to encase them in 10,000 pounds of glass. That year Kunkel received a brass urn filled with ashes and a note.

Sorry, Old Man, here lies the pants…
An attempt to cast the pants in glass
Brought about their demise at last.

The urn now graces Larry Kunkel's fireplace mantel.

DUMB JOCKS

> *"Did I say that?"*

"The doctors X-rayed my head and found nothing."

—Dizzy Dean, Hall of Fame pitcher, after getting beaned

"Sure I've got one. It's a perfect 20–20."
—Duane Thomas, Dallas Cowboys running back, on his IQ

"My grandmother told me it was good for colds."
—Kevin Mitchell, outfielder, on why he eats Vicks VapoRub

"He's a guy who gets up at six o'clock in the morning regardless of what time it is."
—Lou Duva, boxing trainer, on heavyweight Andrew Golota

"Are you any relation to your brother Marv?"
—Leon Wood, basketball player, to announcer Steve Albert

"Better make it six—I can't eat eight."
—Dan Osinski, pitcher, when asked if he wanted his pizza cut into six or eight slices

"Left hand, right hand, it doesn't matter. I'm amphibious."
—Charles Shackleford, North Carolina State basketball player

POTTY MOUTH

*The city of Amsterdam in the
Netherlands, has toilets
that actually talk.*

Artist Leonard van Munster has
created a toilet that gives advice, warns of
germs, and makes fun of you for not washing your hands. It's been installed in the
Café de Balie bathroom…and anyone
who makes a pit stop there will get

an earful. The toilet, which is
wired with sensors connected to
a computer, senses what's happening in the room and responds
accordingly. One reporter heard a
female voice tell him, "You might consider sitting down next time." The next person
was given this warning: "The last visitor did
not take heed of basic rules of hygiene."
Those who think they can sneak off to
the bathroom for a cigarette get a big
surprise when the toilet suddenly starts
coughing and warns them of the
hazards of smoking.

EXTREME IRONING

A strange new sport is born.

One sunny afternoon in 1997 Englishman Phil Shaw looked at his pile of wrinkled clothes and wondered how could he stay inside ironing on such a beautiful day. That's when he decided to combine his least favorite chore with his favorite pastime, rock climbing.

Not long after his first ironing adventure, Phil, known in extreme ironing circles as "Steam," convinced his roommate, "Spray," to join him. While the two ironers practiced their sport, they refined the rules of competition and recruited new athletes for ironing while rock climbing, sailing, and even scuba diving. And it took off: In 2002, 80 different teams from 10 different countries competed in the Extreme Ironing World Championship.

ICE CREAM DREAMS

*Find out what your favorite flavor
reveals about your personality.*

VANILLA: If you love vanilla ice cream, you are a very busy person. You are a social butterfly and love to hang out with your friends. And you never, *ever* miss a party.

BUTTER PECAN: If you love butter pecan ice cream, you are probably the most organized person you know. "Be prepared" is your motto. You love it when a plan comes together.

CHOCOLATE CHIP: If you love chocolate chip ice cream, you are ambitious. You love to win, but you're always fair. You're generous and appreciative, and always the life of the party.

STRAWBERRY: If you love strawberry ice cream, you are a thoughtful and logical person who prefers to work behind the scenes. People might think you're shy, but your pals know that you're an exceptionally kind and loyal friend.

ROCKY ROAD: If you love rocky road ice cream, you are charming and practical. You love the finer things in life, and most of the time you are really outgoing and friendly. But you can become very fierce during a competition. Why? You totally expect to win.

PACKRATS

Who are the most infamous hoarders in history?

NORMAL BEGINNINGS

Homer and Langley Collyer were born into a wealthy New York family in the 1880s. Their father was a well-known doctor and their mother an opera singer. Both boys were raised to be gentlemen and scholars. Homer became an engineer and musician, while Langley was a lawyer. They lived and prospered together in a luxurious three-story mansion in Harlem. And then something snapped.

By 1910 Harlem was becoming a rough, crime-ridden neighborhood. And the worse it got, the more the Collyer brothers retreated into their home. They boarded up the windows, booby-trapped the doors, and shut off their utilities. Then they stopped going out in the daytime and started wandering the neighborhood after midnight. They dug through trash cans for food, gathered water from a pipe four blocks from their home, and began collecting strange stuff—car parts, sewing machines, mannequins, rusted bicycles, broken baby carriages, and junk for their boobytraps. (Langley built a system of booby traps that would dump mountains of trash on top of any intruder.)

HERMIT HIDEOUT

For 33 years, the hermits of Harlem lived behind closed doors, never letting anyone into their lives. Even when Homer became blind and paralyzed from a stroke, they stayed hidden inside their fortress. Langley, convinced Homer's sight would return if he just ate enough oranges, began stockpiling newspapers—thousands and thousands of them—for Homer to read when he regained his sight.

OPEN SESAME

On March 21, 1947, the police received a call that there was a dead man in the Collyer home. It took them more than 24 hours to dig through the trash to get in—every door and window they pried open was fortified by mountains of magazines, broken furniture, suitcases, chandeliers, and trash. They finally found Homer, dead in his chair (he had died of starvation). But where was Langley?

The search began. Every room in the house was crammed floor to ceiling with an outrageous collection of rubbish that included an X-ray machine, dressmakers' dummies, medical specimens in jars, a horse buggy, two pipe organs, a cache of weapons, and 14 grand pianos. Tunnels and crawlspaces were carved into the mountains of junk. Finally, after 18 days of searching, the police found Langley, only a few feet from his brother, buried under a ton of trash—a victim of one of his booby traps. He had died trying to deliver his brother's dinner.

THE STUFF

In the end, 136 tons of trash were hauled away. The Collyer mansion was torn down and turned into a parking lot, but the Collyer legend lives on. Even today, New York City firefighters who get an emergency call to a junk-jammed apartment say, "We got another Collyer."

FASHION POLICE

You can't wear that! It's too weird!

CRIME: In 1750 Jonas Hanway was one of the first men to carry an umbrella in London. Before that time only women carried them.

PUNISHMENT: People on the streets jeered at him.

CRIME: John Hetherington wore the world's very first top hat (also on the streets of London) in the 1800s.

PUNISHMENT: He was arrested for "frightening the public" and fined £50 (today's equivalent: $2,500).

CRIME: In 1907 Australian swimming star Annette Kellerman wore a one-piece bathing suit that revealed her knees and exposed her elbows.

PUNISHMENT: She was arrested for indecent exposure.

THE ELEPHANT MAN

He's been called the saddest man who ever lived. A hundred years after his death, his memory lives on.

Joseph Merrick was born in Leicester, England, in August 1862. At two, the tumors that would disfigure him began to grow. A hunk of flesh that hung from his forehead resembled an elephant's trunk, which gave him his nick-name—the Elephant Man. He had a deformed nose and a hand that looked like a fin, and his body was hung with sacs of wrinkled skin. People called him a monster, but Merrick was an intelligent, gentle person who loved to read and write poetry.

When a popular surgeon named Frederick Treves gave him a home at Whitechapel Hospital in London, Merrick became famous. The toast of London society came to visit him, marveling at the beautiful soul that lived beneath the hideous face. The Elephant Man, whose spine was so twisted he could barely walk, died in his sleep in 1890. He was 27 years old.

SCARY JOKES

These jokes are monstrous!

Q: What do you call a haunted chicken?
A: A poultry-geist

Q: What's a ghost's favorite road?
A: A dead end

Q: Why do vampires brush their teeth?
A: To get rid of bat breath

Q: What do you call a ghost's mom and dad?
A: Transparents

Q: Who should you call when a pumpkin dies?
A: The next of pump–kin

Q: Where do ghosts play tennis?
A: On a tennis corpse

Q: What would you call the ghost of a door-to-door salesman?
A: A dead ringer

Q: How do vampires travel?
A: By blood vessel

Q: What do you get when you cross a were-wolf with a snowball?
A: Frostbite

TONGUE-TIED PROFESSOR

This is what happens when your brain
runs faster than your tongue.

Reverend William Archibald Spooner (1844–1930) was Dean of New College in Oxford, England. He was a short albino with a head too big for his body. But it wasn't his looks that set him apart from others—it was the way he mixed up his words.

He once fumbled a toast to Queen Victoria when he raised his glass and said, "We must drink a toast to our queer old dean." And during a wedding, Spooner told the groom, "Son, it is now kisstomary to cuss the bride."

Reverend Spooner made so many memorable tongue-twisting mistakes that the tendency was named after him.

SPOONERISMS

He Meant To Say...	But He Said...
You have wasted two terms.	"You have tasted two worms."
Which of us in his heart has not felt a half-formed wish?	"Which of us in his heart has not felt a half-warmed fish?"
Is the dean busy?	"Is the bean dizzy?"
Pardon me Madam, this pew is occupied. May I show you to another seat?	"Mardon me padam, this pie is occupewed. May I sew you to another sheet?"

GERM WARFARE

Watch out! They're everywhere!

IN THE BATHROOM...

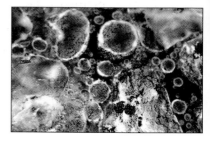

• Every time you flush, water mists into the air and 600,000 bacteria land on everything within six feet of the bowl, including your toothbrush, makeup, hairbrush, and towel.

• Also living in your towels: bacteria and fungus from dead skin.

• One bacteria cell in your loofah can sprout into a billion overnight.

IN THE LIVING ROOM...

• Your couch is crawling with dust mites.

• The household dust on your shelves and coffee table is mostly dead skin.

• Old newspapers are covered in bacteria.

• Watch out for doorknobs and telephones! Danger! Danger! Viruses!

IN THE KITCHEN...

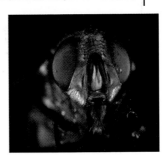

- Your sink is germ heaven. Especially for deadly bacteria like *salmonella* and *campylobacter*.

- Use dishtowels once and bacteria begin growing immediately.

- *Yersinia* bacteria, which causes diarrhea, can be found inside your refrigerator.

- Bacteria from raw meat and unwashed produce live on your cutting board.

IN THE BEDROOM...

- As many as two million dust mites can call one double bed home.

- Dust mites and spiders love the inside of a closet.

- Watch out for your computer keyboard and mouse! Danger! Danger! Viruses!

ON YOUR PETS...

- Dogs can carry salmonella, ticks, fleas, poison oak, and poison ivy.

- Cats can carry parasites like ring worm, roundworm, and *toxoplasma*.

LUCKY FINDS #2

Some people have all the luck...like these guys.

FOUND: A winning ticket
WHERE: In a cactus tree
THE STORY: Evans Kamande, a 17-year-old Kenyan, was playing in a park in Nairobi when suddenly he had to "go." So he found a spot—a nearby cactus tree—and noticed a little box stuck in the fork of the plant's branches. Inside the box: the winning ticket in a treasure hunt sponsored by a local radio station...worth $5,000!

FOUND: A legendary baseball
WHERE: Grandma's attic
THE STORY: In 1996 a New Jersey kid named Mark Scala told his 87-year-old grandmother that he wanted to be Babe Ruth for a school project. She remembered that her late husband had won a signed Babe Ruth baseball back in 1927 when he made the all-state baseball team. Sure enough, they found the ball in an old box up in her attic and were stunned to find out it was the ball from Babe Ruth's very first home run in Yankee Stadium. They sold it in 1998 for $126,500.

THE FIND: A precious gem

WHERE: A mine in North Carolina

THE STORY: Ten-year-old Larry Shields was poking through a bucket of dirt that had been thrown away by a commercial gem mine near his home. He found an interesting rock and decided to keep it because he "liked the shape." Good idea—it turned out to be a 1,061-carat sapphire worth more than $35,000.

THE FIND: A Wendy's cup worth $200,000

WHERE: In the garbage

THE STORY: A sharp-eyed trash collector named Craig Randall from Peabody, Massachusetts, was loading some garbage into his truck when he spotted a Wendy's contest cup sticking out of a trash bag. "I won a chicken sandwich the week before," he said later, "and I figured, hey, I'd get some fries to go with it." When he peeled off the sticker he found a message that read, "Congratulations. You have won $200,000 towards a new home."

THE FIND: The Declaration of Independence

WHERE: Inside a picture frame

THE STORY: In 1989 a Philadelphia man paid $4 for a painting at a flea market, just because he liked the frame. As he was removing the picture from the frame, a piece of folded-up paper fell out. It was a copy of the Declaration of Independence, yellowed with age but otherwise in good condition. The man took it to Sotheby's auction house, where it was found to be one of the original copies from 1776. It sold for a cool $8.14 million.

BABYSITTER TOPS THE CHARTS

Davy Crockett's niece was only a teenager when she wrote America's best-known lullaby.

I n 1872 a 15-year-old girl named Effie Crockett was babysitting a very fussy baby. Trying to calm him down, Effie sang a tune, using the words to an old nursery rhyme. The song worked like a charm. Later, when Effie was given a banjo for Christmas, she plucked out the melody for her music teacher. He liked it so much he sent her to a music publisher in Boston, who liked it, too. Effie

wrote some more verses, the lullaby was published—and it was a hit. Now, more than a hundred years later, babysitters still croon Effie's tune to restless children:

Rock-a-bye baby
on the treetop,
When the wind blows,
the cradle will rock.

When the
bough breaks,
the cradle will fall,
And down will come
baby, cradle and all.

STRANGE AND SILLY RECORDS

What will they think of next?

LEAPFROGGING: In 1991 fourteen students from Stanford University leapfrogged their way to a new world distance record when they hopped 996 miles—almost the entire length of California. (It took them more than 13 days to do it.)

VW BUG CRAMMING: The record was broken on April 29, 2000, when 25 people in Kremser, Austria, stuffed themselves into a new Volkswagen Beetle.

PILLOW FIGHTING: On September 29, 2004, 2,773 warriors (and their pillows) met in Dodgeville, Wisconsin, for the largest pillow fight in history.

WHOOPEE CUSHIONSITTING: In March 2004, 3,614 people simultaneously sat down on whoopee cushions for the biggest-ever whoopee fart-a-thon.

GROUCHO-ING: On June 2005, the Toukey Junior Rugby Club set a new world record for the largest "Groucho Gathering" when 1,437 members of the team crowded onto Darren Kennedy field in NSW, Australia wearing Groucho Marx–style glasses, noses, and moustaches.

DID YOU KNOW?

A *few odd facts to entertain your friends and family.*

• After the Pilgrim ship *Mayflower* sailed to America, it was taken apart and made into a barn.

• Benjamin Franklin invented the rocking chair.

• A whistle sounds louder just before it rains.

• The electric chair was invented by a dentist.

• Shelby Park, born on February 10, 2001, was the first baby to have her birth broadcast live on the Internet.

• Most lipstick contains fish scales.

• In 1996 the Boy Scouts created the new "Public Relations Skills" merit badge. (It has a cell phone on it.)

• Some women in Costa Rica decorate their hair with chains of glowing fireflies.

• In Leonardo da Vinci's famous portrait, Mona Lisa has no eyebrows.

• While it was being developed, the Segway scooter had a top secret code name: Ginger.

• President Andrew Jackson believed the earth was flat.

• Alexander Graham Bell, inventor of the telephone, never called his wife or mother…because they were both deaf.

ROYAL PIG OUT

If you could eat anything you wanted...

VITELLIUS (AD 15–69). This Roman emperor once served 2,000 fish and 7,000 birds at one single feast. His strangest, most famous dish—called "The Shield of Minerva"—consisted of fish livers mixed with peacock brains, tossed with flamingo tongues and the guts of lamprey eels.

HELIOGABALUS (AD 203–222). Only 14 when he became emperor of Rome, he loved to throw huge feasts. Favorite dishes were made of camel's heels, small rodents, and powdered glass. He once served 600 roasted ostriches (with brains), and then dropped so many roses from a false ceiling that some guests drowned in the blossoms.

NEBUCHADNEZZAR II (605–562 BC). He built the Hanging Gardens of Babylon—one of the Seven Wonders of the Ancient World. But this king had much simpler tastes than the Romans. He ate grass. Why? According to legend, he thought he was a goat.

BODY PARTS

*Some famous people didn't go to their graves
with all of their parts. Here's why.*

MISSING BODY PART: Albert Einstein's brain
FOUND: Under a kitchen sink in Kansas.
HOW IT GOT THERE: Einstein had asked that his
friend Dr. Harry Zimmerman examine his brain after he
died. So during the autopsy following Einstein's death in
1955, pathologist Dr. Thomas Harvey removed Einstein's
brain, cut it into 200 pieces, and gave some of it to Zim-

merman as Einstein
had requested. But
Harvey took the
rest to his home in
Lawrence, Kansas.
For the next 40
years, Harvey
stored Einstein's
brain in jars filled
with formaldehyde
under his kitchen
sink, occasionally
giving out speci-
mens to research
scientists. One sci-
entist kept his por-
tion of Einstein's
brain in his refrigerator in a jar marked "Big Al's Brain."

MISSING BODY PART: Galileo's middle finger
FOUND: In an Italian museum
HOW IT GOT THERE: Galileo
Galilei was an Italian scientist who
made important discoveries in physics
and astronomy. In 1737, nearly a century after his death, Galileo's body
was being moved from a storage closet
to a mausoleum, and a nobleman

named Anton Francesco Gori cut off three fingers as a
souvenir. The middle finger was eventually acquired by
the Museum of the History of Science in Florence, Italy.
(The other two fingers are in a private collection.)

MISSING BODY PART: Buddha's teeth
FOUND: In Beijing, China, and Taipei, Taiwan
HOW THEY GOT THERE: Legend has it that two
teeth found in Buddha's cremated remains after his death
2,400 years ago were taken to temples in the Far East.

MISSING BODY PART: Stonewall Jackson's arm
FOUND: On an old battlefield in Virginia
HOW IT GOT THERE: In 1863, at the height of the
Civil War, Confederate general Jackson was accidentally
shot by his own troops. A bullet hit his left arm, which
then had to be amputated above the elbow. His troops
buried the arm in a nearby field, complete with a reli-
gious ceremony and a marble tombstone. When Jackson
died from complications eight days later, the rest of him
was buried in Lexington, Virginia.

GHOSTLY HITCHHIKERS

Here are three good reasons
not to pick up hitchhikers.

THE GHOST OF HIGHWAY 48

In South Carolina, worried motorists reported seeing a young girl carrying a suitcase walking along Highway 48. When the drivers offered her a ride, she told them she was going to visit her sick mother in Columbia. She gave them the address and as they got to the outskirts of Columbia, she suddenly disappeared. One couple who picked her up went to the address and described the girl to a man who lived there. He replied that it was his sister and that she had been killed by a hit-and-run driver in the 1950s while walking to visit their sick mother.

NOW YOU SEE HER—NOW YOU DON'T

Frightened bus drivers in Taiwan have refused to drive to a remote village outside of T'ai-nan because of one ghostly girl. Drivers report stopping at a shadowy area near a sugarcane plantation. A young girl gets on the bus but never gets off. She simply vanishes before the bus gets to town.

RESURRECTION MARY

Nearly every year on the anniversary of her death, a blond-haired, blue-eyed girl in a flowing dress can be

seen standing on the side of Archer Road in Chicago.
Some unsuspecting drivers think she's hitchhiking or in
trouble and offer to give her a ride. They report that she
gets into the car and says, "I have to go home." When
the car nears the gates to Resurrection Cemetery, she
cries, "Here! Stop here!" and simply disappears into
thin air. It seems that Mary had been to a dance at the
O'Henry Ballroom in the 1930s. When she got in a fight
with her boyfriend, she left the dance and started to
walk home. On a curve along Archer Road, near Resurrection Cemetery, Mary was killed by a hit-and-run
driver. For 75 years, Mary's ghost has been doomed to
wander the dark stretch of road looking for "a ride
home."

THE WHO?

Where do rock bands get those strange names?

LIMP BIZKIT. Singer Fred Durst got the idea from his dog, Biscuit, who has a limp.

SMASH MOUTH. Taken from the slang term football players use for any game with a lot of blocking or tackling.

THIRD EYE BLIND. It's said that our "third eye" is the imagined one that gives us a sixth sense. The band felt that when it comes to ESP, most humans are blind.

HOOBASTANK was a word the band members invented when they were in high school. They used it as slang to describe everything.

NICKELBACK got their name from bass player Mike Kroeger, who once worked at Starbucks in Vancouver. At the time, most coffee drinks cost $2.95, $3.95, or $4.95. Kroeger got so used to saying, "Here's your nickel back," that when the band was trying to come up with a name, all he could think of was the phrase "nickel back."

THE WHO. The group, first called The High Numbers, was looking for a new name. Every time someone came up with an idea, they jokingly asked, "The *who*?" Finally a friend said, "Why not just call yourselves 'The Who'?" So they did.

LIZARD MAN

Erik Sprague loves lizards. In fact, he loves them so much that he has spent almost 650 hours (spread over 10 years) in tattoo parlors, transforming himself into a "lizard man." Some of the changes: Sprague was one of the first people to have his tongue surgically forked like a lizard's. Then he had little Teflon balls implanted in his brow. He went on to have his face, eyelids, and most of his body tattooed and pierced to make him look even more lizardlike.

Sprague, who was a National Merit Scholar finalist, now tours in his own "freak" show, where he eats fire, swallows swords, gobbles live worms, and shoots darts out of his nose. His plans for the future? A tail implant.

RIDICULOUS RECORDS

LONGEST DISTANCE RUN BACKWARD

In 1984 Arvind Pandya of India ran backward 3,178 miles, from Los Angeles to New York, in 107 days.

FARTHEST SPAGHETTI NOSE BLOW

On December 16, 1998, with a single blow, Kevin Cole of Carlsbad, New Mexico, blew a strand of spaghetti out of his nose for a record distance of 7.5 inches.

BIGGEST BUBBLE GUM BUBBLE

Susan Montgomery Williams claimed her fourth world record for the biggest bubble gum bubble in 1994 when she blew a monster bubble larger than a basketball—23 inches in diameter—with just three pieces of Bubble Yum gum. Williams claimed her first world record for a bubble gum bubble in 1970 when her 19-inch bubble won her a lifetime's supply of gum.

FASTEST RUMPJUMP

David Fisher of Chicago, Illinois, set a world record in 1998, when he "rumpjumped" 56 times in one minute. What's a rumpjump? Jumping over a jumprope with only your butt.

TALLEST GOLF BALL TOWER

On October 4, 1998, Don Athey of Bridgeport, Ohio, broke the record for building a golf ball tower when he stacked nine balls on top of each other without using any kind of glue.

GREATEST TONGUE-TIE

On January 26, 1999, Al Gliniecki of Gulf Breeze, Florida, tied 39 cherry stems into knots in a record three minutes... using his tongue.

LONGEST DOMINO SETUP

China's Ma Li Hua single-handedly set up the greatest number of dominoes ever—303,628 tiles snaked through a massive maze that covered the floor of the Singapore Expo Hall in Singapore. And then, on August 18, 2003, she toppled them. (All but seven of the dominoes fell over.)

MOST GLASSES BALANCED ON CHIN

On April 26, 2001, Ashrita Furman of New York City balanced 75 pint beer glasses on his chin for 10.6 seconds.

BLACK HOLES

We can't see them. We can't feel them.
But we know they're there.

WHAT ARE THEY?

The bigger a star, the stronger its force of gravity. When a big star explodes (astronomers call that a *supernova*), its dust is scattered throughout the universe. All that's left is a gigantic gravitational force called a *black hole.*

A black hole is like a cosmic vacuum cleaner that sucks everything into it, even other stars. How do we know black holes are out there? Astronomers can see the swirling gases of other stars being sucked toward the blackness. It looks like water going down a drain.

The swirling gases around a black hole go so fast that they get superheated. This causes them to give off X-rays. That was the clue that led to the discovery of the first black hole. In 1970 astronomers detected X-rays coming from an area near a distant star. They expected to find another, even bigger star. But the area emitting the X-rays didn't shine—it was pitch black and 10 times bigger than our sun. Astronomers named the mysterious black spot Cygnus X-1.

BLACK HOLE FACTS

• Black holes can grow. The more stars they swallow, the bigger they get.

• Black holes can swallow *other* black holes.

• There is a black hole right at the heart of our own galaxy, the Milky Way. *Gulp!*

TRY IT...
YOU'LL LIKE IT!

RAT-A-TOOEY

Quang Li-Do has been catching and eating rats for 30 years. He likes them so much that he opened a restaurant in Canton, China, that specializes in rat cuisine. Every year the Jailu Restaurant serves more than 7,500 rats to its satisfied customers!

SALSA STINGER

Some people can't live without chocolate. Others love cheese. But Rene Alvarenga of Intipucá, El Salvador, has a very different craving—scorpions. Live ones! Every day, he snarfs down 20 to 30 of them. He claims to have eaten more than 35,000 in his lifetime.

ROACH BEEF

Entertainer Ken Edwards will do anything for attention. He once stuffed 47 live rats into a pair of pantyhose—while he was wearing them. Then, on March 5, 2001, on live TV, he attempted to break a world record by eating 36 cockroaches in one minute. (He did it!)

MAKE A OUIJA

Want to know what the future holds? Ask the Ouija.

WHAT IS IT? Communicating with "spirits" was a big fad in 19th-century America. Starting in the 1890s you could buy talking boards—called Ouija boards—to speak to them. One manufacturer, Charles Kennard, claimed the board itself told him the word *ouija* was Egyptian for good luck. Another, William Fuld, said the name was a blend of the French and German words for "yes"—*oui* and *ja*. Whatever it means, millions of people have given themselves creepy thrills playing with Ouija boards. Do they really work? You decide.

WHAT YOU NEED TO MAKE ONE:

- A sheet of white cardboard or art board
- Colored pens or pencils
- A small jar or glass
- Lots of imagination

BEFORE YOU BEGIN:

1. Be sure to leave lots of room around the edges of your board so that the pointer doesn't fall off when it moves to a symbol.

2. It is very important that your board is flat and smooth so the pointer can slide easily across it.

DESIGNING THE BOARD:

1. Write the entire alphabet. You can arrange the letters across the top, across the bottom, in a circle, or in any other way you wish.

2. Write the numbers 0 through 9.

3. Write the words YES, NO, HELLO, and GOOD-BYE.

4. Decorate your board.

THE POINTER OR *PLANCHETTE*:

1. Use the small, clean jar or glass as your pointer.

2. Place it upside down on the board with your fingers on the bottom and ask the "spirits" your question. The glass will move, seemingly on its own, to spell out answers.

DISAPPEARING ACTS

Now you see them...now you don't.

THE LOST COLONY. In 1587, more than 100 men, women, and children traveled from England to Roanoke Island off North Carolina's coast and established the first English settlement in North America. Within three years, they disappeared. The colony's leader, Governor John White, had sailed back to England for supplies, and when he returned he found the fort empty of people and their belongings. The only clue to their whereabouts was the word *CROATOAN* carved into a post, with letters *CRO* carved into a nearby tree.

White and others searched for the lost colonists (including his granddaughter, America's first English baby, Virginia Dare)...but to no avail. Their disappearance remains a mystery. However, nearly 200 years later, British explorer John Lawson described a meeting with descendants of the Croatoan tribe. Many of them spoke English and were fair-haired. Could they have been descended from members of the lost colony?

THE VANISHING BATTALION. Three soldiers from a New Zealand field company witnessed the disappearance of an entire army battalion in World War I. It was 1915 and the soldiers watched as the Royal Norfolk Regiment marched up a hill at Suvla Bay, Turkey. A low-lying cloud covered the hill and the regiment marched straight into it. When the cloud lifted into the sky, the battalion of 267 men had disappeared. Their bodies were never found. There were no survivors. They did not turn up as prisoners of war. The entire battalion had simply vanished.

THE DISAPPEARANCE OF DAVID. It was a crisp fall day in September 1880 when David Lang headed off across the pasture to check on his horses. His children, George and Sarah, were playing in the yard of their Tennessee farm. Lang's wife, Emma, stood on the front porch, watching him go. David paused to wave at their friend Judge August Peck, who was trotting up the road in his horse and buggy. Seconds later, David Lang—in full view of his wife, his children, and the judge—disappeared in midstep. Emma screamed, thinking he had fallen into a hole. Everyone rushed to the spot where David had vanished, but there was no hole. They searched the area and found nothing. David was gone, never to be seen again. The Lang children later reported that a 15-foot circle of grass around the spot where their father had disappeared had wilted and turned yellow. Could that have had something to do with his disappearance? Many people believe it was hoax...but no one knows for sure.

TASTE THE MUSIC

Believe it or not, some people can actually say,
"I like that song. It tastes like chocolate."

I magine every time you hear the phone ring…you taste spaghetti sauce. Or whenever you see the number three, it's blue. There are people who see colors when they hear music. And there are other people who not only see colors, but also taste sounds.

This strange ability has a name—*synesthesia*. It's from the Greek words for "together" and "perception," and means that the part of your brain that sees or hears

mixes with the part of your brain that tastes or smells. As unusual as this sounds, one in 2,000 people has the condition.

One Swiss musician says that an F sharp makes her see violet and a C makes her see red. Minor chords makes her mouth taste sour or salty. Major chords make her mouth taste bitter or sweet. Some sounds have weird tastes like mown grass; others are as delicious as creamy milk.

THE HENGES

STONEHENGE is a circle of giant stones that stand on a plain in Great Britain. They align with the sun, moon, and stars and are estimated to be 5,000 years old. Who put them there? What are they for? Archaeologists believe it may have been an astronomical observatory, but no one really knows.

CARHENGE is a replica of Stonehenge created from vintage American automobiles. It juts up from the Nebraska plains on Highway 87 just outside the town of Alliance. Six local families at a reunion decided to build it in 1987. Why? Only they know for certain.

UFO CRASH SITE

Something fell out of the sky near Roswell, New Mexico, on July 8, 1947. Was it a flying saucer? A test plane? Here's what happened that week:

- **Friday:** Jim Ragsdale and Trudy Truelove claim to have seen a flying saucer crash into the desert and strange bodies—four to five feet tall—inside the wreckage.

- **Saturday:** Ragsdale and Truelove witness three army trucks hauling away all of the evidence from the crash site.

- **Sunday:** Local rancher William "Mack" Brazel hears about the crash and gives Major Jesse Marcel at Roswell Air Force Base some strange litter he found in the area. The scraps of metal cannot be cut or burned.

- **Monday:** Mortician Glenn Dennis gets an odd request from an Air Force officer for baby caskets. A nurse tells him she's just helped doctors autopsy strange little bodies.

- **Tuesday:** Base commander Colonel Blanchard issues a press statement: "We have in our possession a flying saucer."

- **Wednesday:** Blanchard's superior officer, General Roger Ramey, says no, the wreckage is just a weather balloon.

- **1970:** Retired Major Jesse Marcel comes forward and says that what he saw back in 1947 was no weather balloon! So, was it a flying saucer? What do *you* think?

UFO CENTRAL

One of the government's most secret locations.

Area 51—also known as Groom Lake—is part of Nellis Air Force Range in southern Nevada. It's a top-secret military base said to be a test-site for performing experiments on captured alien spacecraft. Want to see strange lights and hear weird sounds? Go there.

• Nevada State Highway 375, which runs south of Area 51, has been nicknamed "The Extraterrestrial Highway." Why? Many UFOs have been spotted along this lonely stretch of desert road.

• The stories about Area 51 were mostly just legend... until 1989 when respected scientist Bob Lazar came forward. Lazar told reporters that, in an attempt to unlock its secrets, he had actually worked on an alien spacecraft in 1988.

• Extra-terrestrials have short, gray bodies with almond-shaped eyes.

IT CAME FROM WAY OUT THERE

Falling stars and unidentified flying objects bring some pretty weird gifts.

STAR JELLY

Have you ever watched a falling star or a meteor rocket through the night sky? Most of them burn up in the atmosphere. But some actually hit the earth. Many people who have gone to the places where meteors hit report finding an odd, gooey substance that they call "star jelly." Unfortunately it evaporates pretty quicky, so it's hard to study. Some scientists think this jelly could be *nostoc*, an extremely adaptable type of blue-green algae that grows in clumps in the soil or floats on water. Others think the jelly might be an organism called "slime mold," which grows on the ground and can be

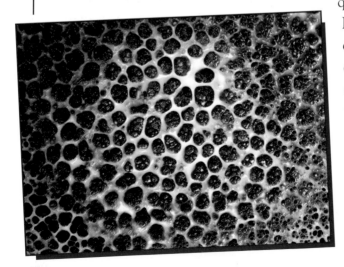

quite large. But whatever it is, no one has yet explained why this strange jelly appears where a meteor has fallen.

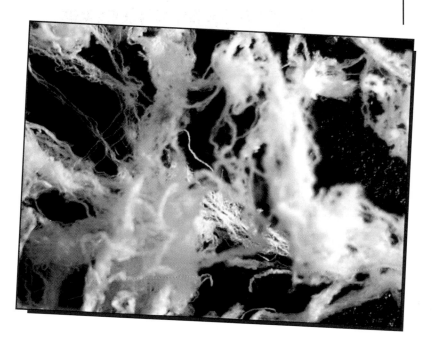

ANGEL HAIR

It is white and silky and looks like spiderwebs floating in the air. Dubbed "angel hair" by those who've seen it, these silky fibers generally appear during the sighting of a UFO. In October 1952, in the village of Oloron, France, high school superintendent Jean-Yves Prigent, his wife, and children, spied a cigar-shaped flying object hovering over their town surrounded by 30 smaller flying saucers. Ten days later 100 people saw the same thing in the town of Gaillac. Both times a substance like "angel hair" fell from the saucers. But when people tried to gather up the silky hair, it turned to jelly and evaporated into thin air.

THE GREEN CHILDREN OF WOOLPIT

Where did these legendary kids come from?

In 12th century England, during the reign of King Stephen, two very strange children were found alone near the town of Woolpit. Workers harvesting in a field heard the cries of a young boy and girl and found them huddled in an open pit, crying. But these were no ordinary children. They spoke a language that no one understood and they were dressed in clothes of an odd metallic material. Stranger still was the color of their skin—green!

The two green children were taken to the home of a man named Richard de Calne. It was difficult for de Calne to get them to eat or drink anything (all they would eat were beans, and only beans that were freshly cut from the beanstalks). The boy soon became ill and died, but the girl survived.

As she grew older and learned English, the green girl was finally able to tell her story, which was as remarkable as her appearance. She said that she and her brother had come from a place that had no sun. All the people there were green and they lived in a land of perpetual twilight. She said her home was across a river of light. When asked how they came to be in the pit, she said that they had heard bells, become mesmerized, and followed the sound of the bells into a cavern. When they emerged, they found themselves in the open pit and were "struck senseless" by the bright lights of our world.

The strange girl's skin faded as she grew up. She married a man from Norfolk, England, but never had any children. And the townspeople never knew if she had come from deep inside our planet or…another world. The green girl died a mystery.

RICE PORRIDGE

It's a breakfast cereal! No—it's a crystal ball.

Every year on February 26, a bowl of porridge is placed on the altar of the Chiriku Hachimangu Shrine in Japan. On March 15 the bowl is removed from the shrine and taken to the local fortune teller, who examines it and predicts what kind of harvest the village will have that year. This tradition has been going on for 1,200 years. In March 2005, the fortune teller spotted something unusual in the bowl of porridge: a crack cut through the shiny surface of the nearly month-old porridge. The fortune teller—Masahiro Higashi—saw the crack, and promptly warned people in the Kyushu area of an upcoming earthquake. Five days later Kyushu was shaken by a quake that measured a strong seven on the Richter scale and damaged more than 600 houses.

CROP CIRCLES

*They appear overnight. What are they
and where do they come from?*

On the night of July 16, 2002, mysterious lights appeared over the fields of Pewsey Downs in Wiltshire, England. The next morning an elaborate pattern shaped like a nautilus shell was carved into the field. Who made it... and why?

Sightings of crop circles go as far back as the 1970s when mysterious patterns that looked like giant pictures suddenly formed in farmers' fields. They have been seen in 29 countries and appear in wheat fields, corn fields, barley fields, rice paddies, and even in ice. They often appear near ancient sacred sites like Stonehenge in England and at crossing points of the earth's magnetic currents.

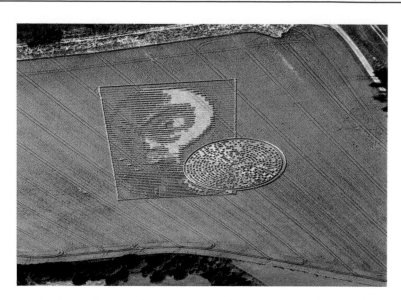

At first, the circles were simple geometric shapes that resembled the ancient Celtic cross. Then they became more elaborate pictograms that looked like ancient rock carvings. Since the 1990s the shapes have begun to mimic computer-generated geometric patterns containing elaborate mathematic equations.

IS IT A HOAX?

In 1991 two 70-year-old men named Doug Bower and Dave Chorley came forward to confess that in the 1970s they had made some of the crop circles using a piece of wood and rope. They even demonstrated on TV how they smashed down the corn to make the patterns. But "hoaxers" have been found to be responsible for only some of the crop circles. The others? Nobody's sure.

On July 8, 1996, a pilot flew over Stonehenge, England, and noted that all was normal below. Fifteen minutes later another pilot reported the formation of a 900-foot crop circle that contained 149 circles. It took surveyors 11 hours just to measure it!

THE REAL MCCOY

So, what makes a true crop circle? Usually the plants in the circles are bent, not broken. Quite often they are crisscrossed into as many as five layers. The circles have precise borders and contain very strong electromagnetic fields—sometimes strong enough to damage a digital camera or a computer. And many eyewitnesses have seen strange globes of light just before or during the formation of the circle.

If you want to actually see one for yourself, head for southern England in the summer. More than 90 percent of reported circles appear there.

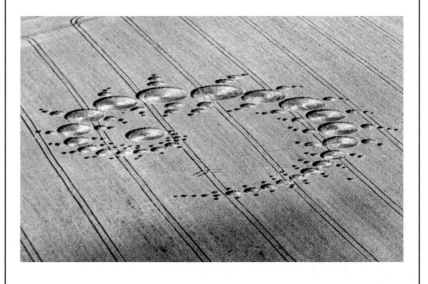

ARE YOU A SLIDER?

Some people have strange powers over electrical appliances. You could be one of them.

When you walk under streetlights or drive by them, do they suddenly turn off or on? If so, you might be a SLIder, a person who appears to have an unusual effect on electrical lights and appliances. With SLIders, Street Lamp Interference (or SLI) doesn't happen once or twice, but all the time. SLIders say that when they are in an extreme emotional state, such as if they're mad, worried, or upset about something, streetlights often turn off.

SLIders also report that when they turn on lamps lightbulbs blow out, and they recount instances of TVs, electronic toys, radios, and CD players going off or on without being touched. SLIders insist that this weird "power" can't be controlled—it just happens.

Hillary Evans, author and paranormal investigator, has even established the Street Lamp Interference Data Exchange as a place for SLIders to share their experiences. So, if lights and TVs are going on and off when you walk by, you may want to get in touch with Evans. She wants to hear your story.

MORE AMAZING COINCIDENCES

R.S.V.P = R.I.P. In 1865 Robert Todd Lincoln was invited to attend a play with his parents. He arrived late to find that his father, Abraham Lincoln, had been assassinated. In 1881 President Garfield invited Robert to join him on a train trip. The president was killed at the station moments before Robert got on board. In 1901 President McKinley invited Robert to a public event. Seconds before Lincoln arrived, McKinley was shot. After that, Robert said he would accept no more presidential invitations, since three had invited him to their assassinations.

HELP! SAVE ME! Roger Lausier was four years old when he got caught in the surf near Salem, Massachusetts. A passing stranger named Alice Blaise rescued him. Nine years later, Lausier was swimming at the same beach when he heard a woman scream for help. Her husband was drowning. He quickly swam out and saved the man's life. Who was the woman? Alice Blaise.

SEA-MAIL. A Japanese sailor named Chunosake Matsuyama was shipwrecked in 1784. Before he and 44 shipmates died of starvation, Matsuyama carved a message on a piece of wood, sealed it in a bottle, and cast it into the sea. A century later the bottle washed up on the shore of a Japanese village—the very seaside village where Matsuyama was born.

THE SKY IS FALLING!

You expect rain, snow, sleet, and maybe even hailstones to come out of the sky...but you'd never expect this!

PENNIES FROM HEAVEN

One day in 1956, pennies rained down on children leaving school in Hanham, England. A year later thousands of 1,000 franc notes fell on the town of Bourges, France. No one ever reported any missing money. It just appeared from "way up there."

TAKE THAT!

Pinar del Río, Cuba, was pelted with mud, wood, glass, and broken pottery in four different rainfalls in 1968.

BLOOD AND GUTS

On August 27, 1968, flesh and blood rained onto an area of land between Cacapava and São José dos Campos, Brazil. The downpour lasted for almost seven minutes!

DUCK!

No one knows why more than a hundred ducks suddenly dropped out of the sky on St. Mary's City, Maryland, in January 1969. The ducks all had broken bones and injuries—but the injuries had happened to them *before* they fell.

FISH AND FROGS AND SNAKES, OH MY!

Reports of fish and reptiles falling from the sky are actually quite common. In 1877 thousands of live snakes dropped out of the sky on Memphis, Tennessee. Scientists speculated that the snakes were swept up by a hurricane, but could never determine where they came from, because there were no hurricanes nearby and no single location could have provided a home to that many snakes.

SPOON BENDING

Want to bend a spoon with your mind? We're not promising you'll be able to do it, but here's a good way to start: have a party!

Pyschokinesis, or PK, is all about mind over matter. People with pyschokinetic powers are said to be able to bend spoons without using any force. The famous spoon-bender Uri Geller claims that it's easy to learn how…and much easier if you are with a group of friends, having fun. Why? Because that's when your mind is in a state of "relaxed inattention"—the perfect time for spoon bending. Here's how:

1. INVITE LOTS OF FRIENDS

It's best to have friends who are curious, fun, and have a great sense of adventure.

2. HAVE LOTS OF SPOONS AVAILABLE

Each spoon bender should take time to find the right spoon. It helps to ask the spoon, "Do you want to bend for me?" Remember, not all spoons want to bend.

3. CLOSE YOUR EYES AND VISUALIZE

Imagine a ball of powerful, endless energy running down your arm and pouring into the spoon.

4. SHOUT LOUDLY AT THE SPOON

Take the spoon, hold it vertically in your hand and

shout, "Bend! Bend! Bend!" Don't skip this step. You've got to let the spoon know who's the boss.

5. LAUGH, GIGGLE, AND BE HAPPY

This is the most important step. When you're having lots of fun, your mind relaxes, making it possible for your spoon to bend.

6. BEND THE SPOON

Hold the spoon in one hand while rubbing it with the other hand. Don't use force—just use laughter. Really! If you worry about bending your spoon, it won't work.

7. BEND-MEISTER

Once you've mastered bending spoons, try bending two forks simultaneously with just your mind. Repeat all of the steps above, except this time you will hold two identical forks at the base, one in each hand. Imagine balls of energy running down your arms and into the forks. Don't forget to laugh.

NUM3ER MADNES5

Adding these random number-facts to your body of knowledge is as easy as one, two, three. (You can count on it!)

• Do you eat meat? If you do, in your lifetime you will devour 14 cows, 880 chickens, 23 pigs, 770 pounds of fish, 35 turkeys, and 12 sheep.

• A "jiffy" is an actual unit of time—it's $1/100$th of a second.

• In a normal eight-hour work day, a typist's fingers travel 12 miles.

• February 2, 2000 (2/2/2000) was the first date to contain only even numbers since August 8, 888 (8/08/888). That's 1,112 years earlier!

• November 19, 1999 (11/19/1999), was the last date containing only odd numbers. The next one will be January 1, 3111 (1/1/3111). That's 1,112 years later!

• Most people remember 20% of what they read, 30% of what they hear, 40% of what they see, 50% of what they say, and 60% of what they do.

• In movies or TV, when a telephone number is spoken or printed, it always begins with 555 because no home phone number begins with that prefix.

• If you watch television for one hour a night between the ages of six and 16, you will have spent eight waking months in front of the TV.

MORE...LOST
AND FOUND

LOST: A rare orchid in New Zealand

FOUND: Under the tent of two botanists who had been searching for it for years—it was completely flattened!

LOST: A little girl in Dover, England, who drifted out to sea on a beach toy (an inflatable set of teeth) in 1994.

FOUND: Rescued by a man floating on an inflatable lobster.

LOST: A Christmas card that was mailed on December 23, 1903, to Elsa Johansson of Sweden.

FOUND: It finally arrived in 1985...82 years later.

SPOOKY SPOTS

Want to meet some real ghosts? Go to...

THE HAUNTED MANSION

One "D" ticket will get you on Disneyland's spookiest ride. Besides the ghosts created by Disney Imagineers, you might see a few real ones. Ghostly uninvited guests at the Haunted Mansion include a man in a tuxedo and an old man with a cane. But the saddest ghost of all is that of a young boy who sits near the exit, crying.

TOYS R US

"Ghosts R Us" might be a better name for this branch of the toy store chain in Sunnyvale, California, said to be haunted by a 19th-century rancher named Johnson. Dolls and toy trucks fly off shelves, books crash to the floor, and baby swings move on their own. Workers say they've felt him brush by or call them by name. Some won't use the ladies' room anymore because Johnson turns on the faucets.

SPANISH MILITARY HOSPITAL

This hospital-turned-museum in St. Augustine, Florida, was built on an ancient Indian burial ground, which may be why it has so many ghosts. Although there are strange growls, nasty smells, floating orbs, and sometimes dripping "ectoplasm" on the walls, director Diane Lane says the ghosts are really very nice—they open doors for her whenever she walks through the building.

EXTREME CASES
Don't laugh. It could happen to you!

HIC!

Charles Osborne could not stop hiccupping. This farmer started hic-ing in 1922, while weighing a pig just before slaughtering it. And for the next 68 years he hic-hic-hiccupped night and day. Sometimes he hiccupped so hard, his false teeth fell out. Over his lifetime he averaged 25 hiccups a minute. That's 430 million hiccups! When he finally stopped hiccupping, Osborne was 96 years old.

AH-CHOO!

Donna Griffiths was just an ordinary 12-year-old schoolgirl in Worcestershire, England, when the sneezing began. It was January 13, 1981—a day she will never forget. Griffiths estimates she sneezed over a million times in the first 365 days. Well-wishers from around the world sent her handkerchiefs and letters suggesting cures. At first she was sneezing at a rate of one sneeze a minute. By the third year, she had slowed to one every five minutes. And finally on September 16, 1983—978 days later—Griffiths stopped sneezing.

ROYAL WEIRDOS

Lifestyles of the rich and strange.

LIONEL WALTER ROTHSCHILD, 2nd Baron de Rothschild (1868–1937), drove a carriage drawn by four zebras. He also had a pet bear that liked to slap women on the butt, and he once hosted an important political dinner that included 12 impeccably dressed monkeys seated at the dinner table.

FRANCIS HENRY EGERTON, 8th Earl of Bridgewater (1756–1829), was known for giving extravagant dinner parties…for his dogs. The pups arrived dressed in the most fashionable clothing of the day (they even wore little shoes).

LUDWIG II of Bavaria (1845–1886) was an extremely shy man, a king who preferred fantasy to reality. He had imaginary dinners with favorite historical figures, and once brought his horse to dinner in the formal state dining room.

"Mad Ludwig" built fairy tale castles in the Bavarian Alps. Neuschwanstein, which means "new swan stone," is the most famous. The rooms were decorated with scenes from operas by his favorite composer, Richard Wagner. Ludwig made sure his dream house had hot and cold running water on every floor, flush toilets, and a central heating system. The castle was unfinished at the time of Ludwig's death in 1886.

KING FAROUK of Egypt (1920–1965) owned dozens of palaces, thousands of acres of land, and hundreds of cars. And he was a notorious pickpocket. The "Thief of Cairo" stole a pocket watch from Winston Churchill and a ceremonial sword right out of the casket of the Shah of Iran.

SNOOZE CLUES

According to Professor Chris Idzikowski of the Sleep Assessment and Advisory Service, your sleep position reveals your personality type. Which one are you?

1. FETAL: You are a little shy at first, but it doesn't take you long to warm up.

2. LOG: You are easy-going and trusting. You love being the center of activity.

3. YEARNER: You like to check your facts before you make up your mind. Once you've made a decision, you're committed to it.

4. SOLDIER: You are a quiet person, even a little reserved. You set high standards for yourself and others.

5. FREE-FALLER: You are ambitious and outgoing, sometimes even a little foolish. But ultimately, you'll never put yourself in an extreme situation.

6. STARFISH: You are a compassionate friend and good listener. You'd rather not be the center of attention.

Fetal   Log   Yearner   Soldier   Free-faller   Starfish

LAWN-CHAIR LARRY

This truck driver always wanted to fly,
and at the age of 33 he finally did.

On July 2, 1982, Larry Walters tied 45 helium-filled weather balloons to an aluminum lawn chair in his backyard in San Pedro, California. Equipped with a bottle of soda, a camera, a CB radio, an altimeter, and a BB gun (for altitude control), Larry strapped on a parachute and climbed into his "aircraft"—the *Inspiration I*.

Before his friends could untie all the ropes, it broke loose. Seconds later Walters found himself floating at 16,000 feet. Startled pilots alerted air traffic control that a guy in a lawn chair was drifting into the approach to Long Beach airport.

The thin air was making Walters dizzy, so he popped several balloons with his BB gun and tried to land on a golf green. Instead, he got tangled up in some power lines. (He wasn't electrocuted, but he did cause a blackout over Long Beach.) Walters escaped with a $1,500 fine...and his life.

"Since I was 13, I've dreamed of going up into the sky in a weather balloon," Walters said later. "And by the grace of God, I fulfilled my dream. But I wouldn't do this again for anything!"

YOU'VE GOT MAIL

Can't find an envelope? Who cares?

Accprding to government regulations, you can send almost anything through the United States Postal Service, as long as you follow these simple rules:

1. *No dangerous chemicals, explosives, or glass.*
2. *No live animals.*
3. *Apply the correct postage.*

Here are a few things that have actually been sent—unwrapped—but with the correct postage:

• **Money** (wrapped in clear plastic): a quarter, a $1 bill, and a $20 bill.

• **Clothing:** Brand-new tennis shoes; a sock tied to a set of keys.

• **Toys:** A football, a Lego postcard made out of actual Legos, and a toy monkey in a box. (When the box was shaken, the monkey screamed, "Let me out of here! Help! Let me out of here.")

• **Goofy stuff:** A rose, a feather duster, a ski, a roll of toilet paper, and a message in a clear plastic bottle.

• **Food products:** A coconut, a wheel of smelly cheese, a wax peach.

PARTY ANIMALS

When you want to celebrate, what do you do?
Sing songs? Eat cake? When these guys celebrate
they go to strange (and scary) extremes.

BLOCO DE LAMA. Every year during Carnival in Brazil, these people dress up like cavemen, cover themselves in mud, and parade down the streets of the town of Paraty. The sulfurous mud is said to be good for the skin. But most just do it for the fun of it.

LA TOMATINA. The largest food fight on the planet takes place every year in Spain when 240,000 pounds of tomatoes are shipped into the small town of Bunol. More than 30,000 tourists make the journey to Bunol for the chance to hurl tomatoes at each other and be covered from head to toe in red slime.

FLUSHED AND FOUND

Top 20 most unusual items flushed down the toilet.

1. A bedspread
2. A possum
3. A pair of hiking boots
4. Fourteen pairs of men's extra-large briefs
5. False teeth
6. A wig
7. Rubber ducks
8. A rattlesnake
9. A seven-foot-long boa constrictor
10. Piranhas
11. TV remotes
12. An alarm clock
13. An 8-ball
14. Thirty golf balls
15. A bowling ball
16. A baseball bat
17. Twelve glass eyes
18. A bunch of $100 bills
19. A diamond
20. A Timex watch (still ticking…)

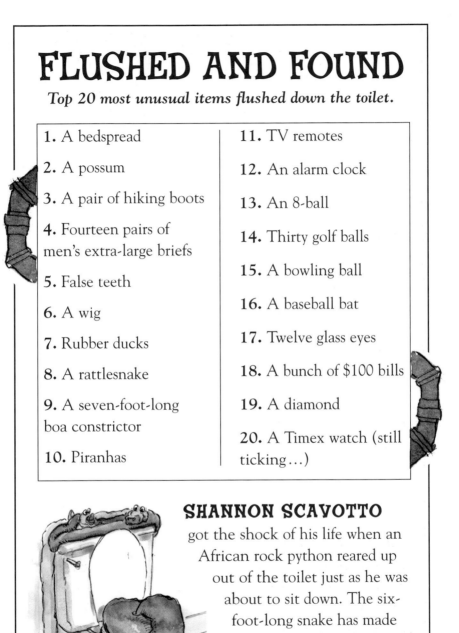

SHANNON SCAVOTTO

got the shock of his life when an African rock python reared up out of the toilet just as he was about to sit down. The six-foot-long snake has made the entire family think twice about using the toilet—especially in the dark.

BRITS AND THEIR "COMPS"

*Welcome to the quirky world
of British competition.*

BOG SNORKELING

Ever since 1985, the town of Llanwrtyd Wells, Wales,
has hosted the Annual Peat Bog Competition. Competitors must swim two lengths of a 60-yard-long, muddy,
reed-filled trench wearing snorkels and flippers. They
can't use any conventional swim strokes, must not touch
the bottom, and have to keep their faces in the muddy
bog. The snorkeler with the fastest time wins.

CHEESE ROLLING

For hundreds of years, Cooper's Hill near Gloucester, England, has hosted an annual cheese roll. Cheese rolling may have started as an ancient fertility rite, but it has evolved into an all-out rollicking race down a very steep and extremely treacherous hill. At the start of the race an 8-pound, 3-inch-thick wheel of cheese is hurled down Coopers Hill. A moment later, the competitors run after the cheese. They never catch the cheese. By the time it reaches the bottom of the hill, the cheese is traveling 70 mph. Runners who are still on their feet when they reach the bottom of the hill (and very few make it that far) are tackled by rugby players to keep them from crashing into the fence at the end of the course. The first runner to cross the finish line gets to keep the cheese.

WORM CHARMING

In 1980 Tom Shufflebotham stunned the world by charming 511 worms out of the ground in 30 minutes at the first World Worm Charming Championships in Nantwich, Cheshire. Since then no one has been able to beat his record. How do you charm a worm? The most successful method is called "twanging"—inserting a four-pronged pitchfork in the ground and twanging it (vibrating it) until the worm crawls out. Under no circumstances can a competitor dig a worm out of the ground.

VAMPIRE BASICS

This simple guide will tell you everything you need to know about how to decide if your next door neighbor is a vampire.

THE TELLTALE SIGNS OF A VAMPIRE

• A vampire casts no reflection. It cannot be seen in a mirror or a photograph.

• A vampire is allergic to sunlight. It can only go out at night.

• Vampires cannot be heard over telephone lines.

• Vampires cannot or will not cross running water.

• Vampires are shape-shifters; they turn into bats, wolves, or wisps of smoke to travel.

• Vampires grow stronger as they get older.

HOW TO PROTECT YOURSELF

Garlic: Hang it around your neck. Rub it on your windows and doors. Garlic severely weakens a vampire.

Cross: Wear a cross around your neck. Crosses burn vampires.

Roses: Plant wild roses in your yard. Most vampires hate them.

Light: Keep your home well lit. A bright light will temporarily blind a vampire.

Hide the welcome mat: Whatever you do, never invite a vampire into your home. It cannot enter your house without your invitation.

STRANGE DEATHS

What a way to go!

SILENT BUT DEADLY

A man whose diet consisted of nothing but beans and cabbage was killed by his own farts. One night, while he was asleep, the noxious gas he "created" hovered over his bed and became so deadly that he never woke up. The three rescue workers called to the scene got sick, too—one even had to be taken to the hospital.

BLOWOUT

Children's entertainer Marlon Pistol was killed when a 20-foot-tall balloon elephant that he used in his act suddenly inflated in his tiny car as he drove along a California highway.

DRUMMED OUT OF TOWN

A Japanese man attempting to win the world record for nonstop drumming was stabbed to death by his neighbor, who just couldn't take one more beat.

HE PASTA WAY

When 150-mph winds hit chef Juan Ruiz's restaurant in Mexico City, he was stabbed through the heart by a flying strand of uncooked spaghetti.

THE LAST WORD

And that's final.

Here lies
the body of
Emily White

She signalled
left and then
turned right.

Here lies
Matthew Mudd,

Death did him
no hurt;

When he was alive he
was only Mudd,

Now he's
only dirt.

Once I
Wasn't.

Then I Was.

Now I ain't
Again.

Harry Edsel Smith
Born 1903
Died 1942

Looked up the
elevator shaft
To see
If the car was on
the way down.
It was.

UGLY IS BEAUTIFUL

Gurning: the art of making ugly faces.

Every year since 1267, the town of Egremont, England, has hosted the World Gurning Championship. Men, women, and children cross their eyes, blow out their cheeks, suck in their noses, or twist their mouths to make the grossest face possible. Ugly is beautiful at the World Gurning Championship. But gurning's not about coming into the contest ugly. Being naturally ugly won't make a competitor an automatic winner. Champion gurners know how to transform their faces into grotesque masks without the help of their hands or artificial aids. (Hint: It helps to be toothless.)

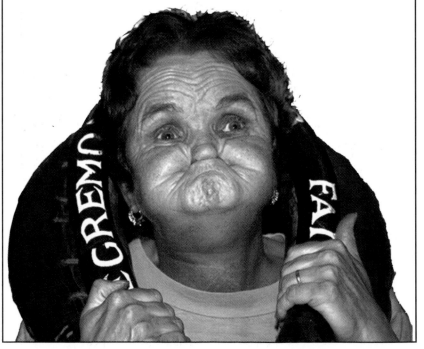

POTTY ON, DUDE!

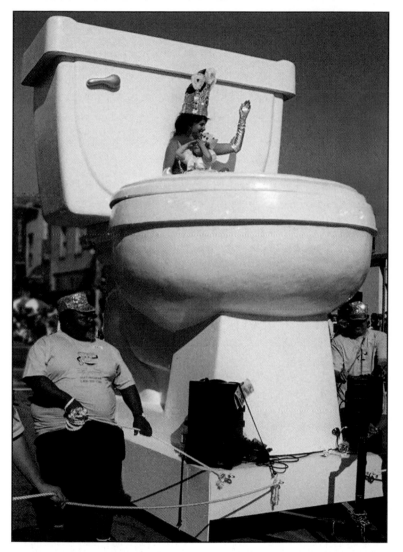

The queen of Pasadena, California's annual Doo Dah Parade is flush with pride as she sits serenely upon her throne and waves to crowds of adoring fans.

PHOTO CREDITS

Uncle John's Bathroom Readers For Kids Only!

Uncle John's Bathroom Reader
For Kids Only!
© 2002. $12.95
288 pages, illustrated.

Uncle John's **Electrifying**
Bathroom Reader For Kids Only!
© 2003. $12.95
288 pages, illustrated.

Uncle John's **Top Secret!**
Bathroom Reader For Kids Only!
© 2004. $12.95
288 pages, illustrated.

Uncle John's **Book of Fun**
© 2004. $12.95
288 pages, illustrated.

To order, contact:
Bathroom Readers' Press
P.O. Box 1117, Ashland, OR 97520
Phone: 888-488-4642 Fax: 541-482-6159
www.bathroomreader.com

THE LAST PAGE

FELLOW BATHROOM READERS
Bathroom reading should never
be taken loosely, so Sit Down
and Be Counted! Join the Bathroom
Readers' Institute. It's free! Just go to
www.bathroomreader.com to sign up. Or
send a self-addressed, stamped envelope and
your e-mail address to: Bathroom Readers'
Institute, P.O. Box 1117, Ashland, Oregon 97520. You'll
receive a free membership card, our BRI newsletter (sent
out via e-mail), discounts when ordering directly through
the BRI, and you'll earn a permanent
spot on the BRI honor roll!

UNCLE JOHN'S NEXT BATH-ROOM READER FOR *KIDS ONLY* IS ALREADY IN THE WORKS!

Is there a subject you'd like to see in our
next *Uncle John's Bathroom Reader* for kids?
Write to us at *www.bathroomreader.com* and
let us know. We aim to please.

Well, we're out of space, and when
you've got to go, you've got to go. Hope
to hear from you soon. Meanwhile,
remember…

Go with the Flow!